… last …

THE
ALMIGHTY
DOLLAR

THE ALMIGHTY DOLLAR

Follow the incredible journey
of a single dollar to see how the
global economy *really* works

Dharshini David

First published 2018 by
Elliott and Thompson Limited
27 John Street
London WC1N 2BX
www.eandtbooks.com

Hardback ISBN: 978-1-78396-338-6
Trade paperback ISBN: 978-1-78396-376-8
eBook ISBN: 978-1-78396-339-3

9 8 7 6 5 4 3 2 1

A catalogue record for this book is available from the British Library.

Typesetting: Marie Doherty
Printed in the UK by TJ International Ltd

For Sophia & Livia

Contents

Introduction

Have you ever wondered why we can afford to buy far more clothes than our grandparents ever could but are less likely to own a home in which to keep them all? Why your petrol bill can double in a matter of months, but never falls as fast? Why our governments ignore some atrocities around the world, but don't hesitate to wade into other conflicts?

Reading the news these days might lead you to wonder whether any of us can really afford to get old any more, or whether there can ever be enough jobs to go round in a time of mass migration.

Behind all of this lies economics. These days it's a dirty word, especially since the crash of 2008. It's become shorthand for a baffling system in which many of us have lost faith. Economists – the financial weather forecasters – have suffered a bad press. They failed to see the storm coming, and when it hit they couldn't work out what needed to be done to repair the damage. Those pulling the strings – the politicians, the faceless corporations – often seem either clueless or, worse, full of dark intent.

Economics is sometimes called the dismal science, but it could also be the *distant* science. The World Economic Forum holds its annual invitation-only gathering of top business and government leaders in Davos, a remote town in the Swiss Alps. The delegates jet in from all over, with the odd Hollywood actor such as Angelina

Jolie or Leonardo DiCaprio roped in to add a little stardust. The term 'Davos man' (and they're still predominantly men) has become slang for a member of the global elite. It's their conversations – held in conference halls, in corridors or over drinks – that underpin the decisions that control all our fates.

The chances of most of us receiving an invitation to Davos are slim but, even if we aren't in the room, we can still understand those conversations – and we do need to understand them. The 'Davos men' might be pulling the strings but knowing how the system works can give us all a little more power. We can exert that power not only by choosing the politicians we vote for, but also through the tiny decisions that we all make every day, wherever we are in the world.

It was a desire to tell people about the strange world of economics, and its implications for us all, that led me to swap a career on a City trading floor for a newsroom. (On a personal level, that's perhaps not the most rational economic decision.) Now, with the fallout of the financial crisis still clouding the picture, I wanted to provide a clearer view of how economic forces shape the world we live in. And so this book was born.

Meet Dennis Grainger. Don't let his mild-mannered appearance fool you: greying, eloquent and smartly turned out, Dennis looks and sounds every inch a retired bank manager from the north-east of England. To look at him you wouldn't guess that he's spent over a decade waging a bitter war on the murky world of finance.

In 1998 Dennis landed a new job at the Sunderland office of British bank Northern Rock. Planning diligently for his future, he saved every penny, hoping to retire within a decade. He didn't qualify for a company pension, so instead he bought shares in his employer's business: for a local lad, what could be safer than a solid local bank? From humble origins in the nineteenth century, Northern Rock had grown to become a national provider of savings accounts and mortgages to millions in the UK. It was trusted; it was part of the establishment.

Dennis's wife might have been concerned when the price of the bank's shares dipped somewhat in 2007, threatening their retirement plans, but Dennis remained confident. That trust was betrayed on 14 September, when Northern Rock admitted it was running low on funds and had to seek an emergency bailout from the Bank of England. Panic ensued. Savers rushed to its seventy-two branches to rescue their life savings. Queues wrapped around the block; the phone lines were jammed. Politicians offered reassurances about the future of the bank, but the queues just kept getting longer, including at a branch just yards from the Bank of England. The first run on a British bank in 150 years was under way. It was an unbelievable sight in the world's financial capital. Behind the scenes, embarrassed politicians and bankers feverishly explored rescue options for what they surreally called Project Elvis.

Within months, the government had taken over the bank, and Dennis's shares, once worth more than £110,000, were worthless. He'd done what too few of us manage to do: he'd saved diligently to provide for his future. But it was all for nothing.

Northern Rock has now become synonymous with the financial crash of 2008 that taught us to expect the unexpected. From the first early signs, most people didn't recognise that disaster was coming – and on an unprecedented global scale. When the crisis imploded, prudent Dennis was among those paying a steep price for the misbehaviour of others, and he continues to fight for compensation from the UK government. It's not just for him; he's spearheaded a campaign on behalf of many former shareholders. A world away from the fat cats pilloried in the press in the wake of the crisis, many of those seeking compensation are the widows or children of former employees who thought Northern Rock was as safe as the houses it financed.

Who is to blame for such a catastrophe? The UK government is the first port of call for redress, but the blame for the crisis that claimed these ordinary people's savings may lie further afield. We might look to the bankers who sidestepped the rules and were relying on dubious funds to bolster their profits. Or we might look to those lenders who approved loans to American consumers who couldn't afford to pay them back. We might wonder how the actions of individuals have contributed to something so vast, and so seemingly out of anyone's control.

To understand fully what happened to Dennis and the millions of others whose prosperity was dented in 2008, we need to look at how the global economy works.

The world as we know it is becoming both smaller and more complex. Seven billion of us live and work on this earth, and we are all vying for the same items in limited supply: food or oil or even smartphones. It's an increasingly interconnected system in which a word from a banker in Washington or Berlin can lead to pensioners in Greece going hungry, or a young man leaving his family to trek across sub-Saharan Africa in search of a better life. This shrinking of the world, or globalisation, often seems like a vast impersonal force, one that works in favour of some but deals harshly with others. And, it seems, we can't escape it.

Eight time zones away in Beijing, Wang Jianlin's experience has been very different from that of Dennis Grainger. Born in Sichuan province in 1954, Wang Jianlin followed his father into the People's Liberation Army, but that family tradition wasn't enough to satisfy him. Instead, within a few decades, he became a property mogul worth billions of dollars, and has gone on to amass a global portfolio including the world's largest movie-theatre chain and priceless Picassos. Not many former Chinese border guards get compared to a James Bond villain, but this erstwhile communist foot soldier has an empire that Blofeld would envy. Wang spent his fortune on Odeon and AMC theatres, enabling Europeans and Americans to enjoy the Hollywood blockbusters that were banned in China. He spent $45 million on a 20 per cent stake in the leading Spanish football club Atlético Madrid, when €1,000 would have bought him a season ticket. It was his purchase of the yacht supplier to the Bond films that led to press comparisons with Fleming's evil super-tycoons. The *Economist* magazine hailed his 'Napoleonic ambition' and his still-trim figure mirrors the 'iron discipline' with which he manages his ventures. For all his upright military bearing, his main aim is to entertain millions around the globe every week. He's not a sportsman, or a film star; he is China's richest man.

Wang is skilled as an entrepreneur and businessperson, but it isn't enough simply to take advantage of the right opportunity. His success has come from riding the tidal wave of global economic changes that we've seen over the past thirty years. As a major manufacturer, investor and, more recently, a mega-consumer, Wang has made the most of those changes, from developing the commercial properties that underpinned China's industrial transformation to backing karaoke centres for its booming urban middle classes. The rise of China is also one of the major political stories of our era. It's a gripping tale – and, as we'll see, in many ways it's linked to what happened to Dennis Grainger.

These are just the stories of two of the billions of people on our planet but they show how we can rise or fall by the forces of the global economy – forces that often seem to be outside our control.

We might think of the global economy as all of the transactions, interactions, purchases and agreements that we understand as trade. Over time, the flow of income generated by those trade relationships accumulates as wealth. The economy, and the forces it contains, are shaped by the actions of individuals – whether at Davos or in a street market in Calcutta – in ways they might not intend.

One thing is certain, however: we are all subject to these forces and, whether we can control them or not, it's important to know how they work, and how they affect our lives.

In London and New York, in Paris and Milan, and even in Beijing, Fashion Week is big business, but we no longer need a couture-sized budget to buy the hottest looks from the catwalk. Within weeks, the designs will be popping up on the racks of our local Primark or Zara. As we browse the aisles, we might notice how many garments are made in the Far East. When we buy from retailers such as these, we're not just scratching our personal fast-fashion itch. The transaction makes us part of a far bigger global story. As we chase low prices and the latest trends, we're transferring income to the other side of the world, to the benefit of others. It's no secret that clothing manufacturers are tapping into cheap labour in Asia. But the story is more complex, because by buying these items we might have contributed to the forces that triggered a financial crisis at home, hurting our own livelihoods and those of our loved ones.

Behind every transaction there is a story. Every pound, euro or yen that we spend tells a tale. With the constant international flux of people, cash and ideas, it can be hard to get a sense of how it all fits together. But we can do so, by unpicking the decisions and the logic behind the transactions – even the seemingly insignificant ones – and tracing their impact and how they are linked.

Imagine all the billions of transactions that take place every day – a housewife in America or Nigeria buying groceries, a French businesswoman banking her profits, an Indian father paying for his daughter's wedding or an Australian buying beer for a barbecue. When we go shopping, if we're outside the USA, the chances are that we're not spending dollars. We might think that the dollar is just one among many currencies; that it's a piece of paper or an electronic transaction that allows us to buy or sell goods in the USA. But we'd be wrong. It's not just another currency. First and foremost, it's the face of American economic power. Like all currencies, the dollar can be seen as the measure of a country's fortunes. We hear politicians and commentators talking about the strength of a nation in terms of its currency: 'the pound fell today'; 'the yen soared'. Of course the dollar is powerful; it represents the most powerful nation on earth. For those on American soil, it also represents the strength of the American dream.

The dollar is also the face of American might, and American interests. A dollar doesn't just bring spending power; it brings influence. Having a dollar – or not having a dollar – can dictate the way people live on the other side of the world. Dollar diplomacy – the use of American investment or loans to influence policy overseas and access foreign markets – has famously been deployed across Latin America, but it's made its presence felt across the world for as long as America has been independent.

The dollar is even more than just a symbol of power and influence, though: it's also one of the most trusted stores of value in the world. Aid workers might find flashing dollars to be the quickest way of securing equipment to ease a humanitarian crisis in areas of great instability. As prices soared in Argentina in 2001–2002 and pesos were rapidly devalued, some wealthier people decided their life savings would be safest stashed under the mattress in dollars. The dollar is secure, and it's therefore a popular substitute currency. Equally, it is a favourite of corrupt businesspeople and politicians everywhere; easily understood, easily spent.

And there's more. The dollar is also the world's 'reserve currency' – we'll find out more about what this means later. Essentially, it's about trust. The dollar is the most trusted currency everywhere, whether it's Japanese banks hoarding their wealth or a market trader bartering in Panama. Even in Soviet Russia, many people preferred the dollar to their own rouble.

Because the dollar is the most trusted currency on earth, it has become a powerful tool in the creation of the global economy that we're all a part of, whether we like it or not. Globalisation works because we have found ways of linking people together – and the dollar is a key part of that. It's the face of global financial stability (and instability); the bedrock for our survival (or not). It's the financial language that underpins all our lives, regardless of the notes and coins we use every day. It signifies how interlinked all our fortunes are. In short, we might view the dollar as the agent of globalisation, doling out prosperity – but not to all.

∽

As the offspring of globetrotting parents, I was conscious of the dollar's omnipresence early on. After all, it's the common language of hotel bills from Brunei to Barbados. Today, the dollar may be best known for keeping the wheels of fortune spinning across the USA, but the name isn't even American. *Thalers* – or *dalers* as they were also known – were silver coins first used in sixteenth-century Bohemia. The name evolved into an English version – 'dollars' – which even made an appearance in Shakespeare's *Macbeth* in 1606. Dollars were used widely, including in Spain and Portugal, and thus made their way to the New World where Spanish conquerors plundered Mexico's silver mines to produce dollar coins. Some of these crept north of the border into British territory, facilitating business where British pounds (or alternative currencies, including tobacco) weren't available. Come independence, the Americans sent the pound the way of tea, and the dollar was fully embraced as the official currency of the USA in 1792.

The rise and rise of the dollar in the twentieth century reflects the rise of the current global order and has coincided with the pre-eminence of the USA. How it gained pole position in the first place appears to have been as much by luck as by design. In the 1930s the Great Depression had weakened the USA and its currency, but then came the Second World War and, as Europe and Japan nursed their wounds, America was poised to broker lasting peace. It set the dollar as the currency of international trade and stability.

The influence of the dollar has grown as globalisation has gathered pace. The Cold War and its aftermath might have offered a chance to challenge it but the collapse of communism and break-up of the USSR created a vacuum, and we can all guess which currency was poised to take advantage of the resulting chaos. Although America's economy makes up less than a quarter of the world's economy, the dollar now crops up in 87 per cent of all transactions involving foreign currencies.

These days, George Washington's face is probably the most reproduced on the planet. It's on the 17 million $1 notes printed every day. 'Dead president' is just one of the many names a dollar bill answers to. Singles, bucks or greenbacks, call them what you will, more than 11.7 billion of them are floating around right now, in wallets, in ATMs, under mattresses or in shop tills – not to mention all the dollars held electronically in banks. Given the dollar's global pre-eminence, perhaps it's not surprising that half the dollar notes in circulation are outside the USA.

It has not been uncommon to hear economists and politicians – particularly America's foes – predicting the decline of the dollar, especially following the crash of 2008. However, the sheer magnitude of the dollar's might remains. It first hit me after I'd been posted to New York in 2006 to present the BBC's financial coverage of Wall Street. That year, an economist shared his predictions for the American housing market on my show. After bubbling comfortably upwards for the past couple of decades, the line on the graph plunged sharply. That was his prediction based on iron-clad evidence and well-tested formulae. It was scary, almost the stuff of conspiracy theory. It was tempting to dismiss it as scaremongering and move on.

But he was right. Millions of Americans had been given mortgages that they couldn't hope to repay. The initial fear was that this might hurt the fortunes of banks on Wall Street, and spending on Main Street, USA, but even as I explained this on the airwaves, the global domino effect was becoming clear. The queues were building up outside Northern Rock and banks from Frankfurt to Beijing were feeling the burn. The quest for profits that had driven an insatiable financial system underpinned the contagion. Governments – or rather taxpayers – had to foot the bill for the damage. International trade collapsed. The scars remain.

A decade on, America is still dominant, and its currency is as popular internationally as ever. The dollar is a safe haven, and every geopolitical storm seems only to reinforce that reputation. China has seen meteoric expansion, but as a superpower it's still hovering in the wings. The dollar remains untainted; in fact, by 2017 it was about 35 per cent stronger against the pound than it had been in 2008. In many ways, a strong dollar is good for America's image. (Although, as we'll see, it can also weaken both the US economy and the economies of other countries.) The currency is the ulti-mate is the ultimate expression of America's political and economic supremacy – and, as we'll see, the ubiquitous dollar also helps to spread the long arm of American law well beyond its borders.

The global crisis underlined how money transcends boundaries; transactions in one country can have repercussions everywhere. Money is both the lubrication that keeps the system running and the glue that binds us together. Like any currency, the dollar's strength is based on faith – some might say blind faith. But without that trust – if no one had confidence in it – the system, and with it society, would collapse.

It is time, then, to follow a dollar around the globe, to grasp its power. Our journey will involve more currencies than just the dollar: euros, rupees and pounds, for example, all come into it. But I hope that by following our money as it changes hands, either physically or electronically, we can shed some light on the nexus of transactions that shapes every aspect of our world. Each scenario is a crucial part of a jigsaw that will reveal exactly how our world works: who really holds the power, and how that affects us all.

We start in suburban Texas: a run-of-the-mill trip to Walmart, one of the world's largest retailers, that keeps Americans fed, clothed and satisfied. One person's impulse buy of a bargain-priced radio sets off an intricate chain reaction, taking a dollar to China, where the radio was made. How can China produce these goods so cheaply, and who benefits? We'll see how dollars fit into China's ambitions in one of the major global stories of our era.

And where is China stashing all its money? Sometimes in the most unlikely of places, including Nigeria, where we head next, to find out why some countries are so interested in splashing their cash overseas, and whether that arises from altruism or greed.

In Nigeria we see how the world's wealth can flow through some countries without benefiting most of their people. Following the dollar in search of a plate of rice to feed Nigeria's booming population, we uncover a similar story in India. India has the fastest-growing major economy of all. So why is the farmer who grew the rice not enjoying those spoils? India has developed in a different way from most other countries and spiced things up, with interesting results.

Powering this economic dynamo requires fuel, and for that, India is sending its dollars off to Iraq, where we'll examine the murky world of black gold. Crude oil is crucial to our survival, and to the supremacy of the dollar. It represents a global order in which all eyes are on Saudi Arabia and the Middle East, but that could change in the coming century. World peace is bad news for Russia, the dollar's next destination. An arms manufacturer can tell a tale or two about his homeland's dysfunctional – but important – dance with the dollar: this is power play on a global scale.

From Russia we head to Berlin, the heart of the EU. The dollar might unite the fifty states of the USA, but Germany, the grande dame of Europe, has had a wholly different experience in Euroland. What makes a currency union work? Why has the euro not overtaken the dollar? And is the UK right to turn its back on the EU? For all the dollar's supremacy, it's still London that's the financial capital of the world, though it might not be substantially different from a casino, with its myriad opportunities to make and lose money. How did those gambles tip us into the biggest financial crisis ever? As the UK puts its future at stake with Brexit, we head back west, where a dollar will once again settle in the pocket of an American, showing how the prosperity of even the world's most powerful nation, one that often stands alone, is inextricably linked with the prosperity of the rest of the world.

The characters and transactions we'll come across are fictitious. But their stories are typical of billions around the globe whose interactions and decisions underpin our fates. The dollar has been on a journey that's revealed how the global economy *really* works, and how Dennis's and Wang's fates are interlinked with that of the rest of us. It's a story of money and of power – but, fundamentally, it's the story of us.

1

Worshipping at the temple of low prices and endless offers

The USA to China

Diapers, bread, milk, juice, apples, chicken . . . the supermarket conveyor belt is a roll-call of Lauren Miller's weekly essentials. It's the family shopping list familiar across suburban America. And tagged on to the end on this occasion: a brand new radio. As the items are scanned by one assistant and packed into paper sacks by another, Lauren reaches into her bag and pulls out a bundle of the most instantly recognisable currency on the planet: the almighty dollar bill. Lauren's grocery shop is a weekly ritual, as is making the most of her budget. Pay rises aren't what they used to be but she still squeezes in the odd luxury. Today, that's a new radio for the kitchen. The price is almost unbelievably low. Everywhere she looks, more bargains vie for her attention in the packed aisles of this cavernous Walmart. As the cashier tells her to have a nice day, she navigates her cart around the squabbling families and lone browsers, out to the parking lot, away from the cacophony of shoppers and the urge to spend.

Every week, close to 100 million Americans undertake a pilgrimage to a similar cathedral of consumption. The item they are most likely to put in their trolley? The humble banana. Not that there's any lack of choice. Pop into the nearest Walmart Supercenter (and with 3,504 dotted across the USA there's likely to be one within a fifteen-minute drive) and up to 142,000 different items – some edible, some not – will line the shelves. It would take some time to browse them all. The biggest Walmart is in Albany, New York. It clocks in at 24,000 square feet: that's four football pitches. Pass the trademark greeters at the door ('Hi, how you doin'?') and the shelves are piled high with food, toys, electronics, tools, clothes, items for the car . . .

It's the ultimate one-stop bargain basement shop. Signs promising EVERYDAY LOW PRICES pepper the brightly lit aisles and temptation is everywhere. The price tags make the products irresistible, promising untold satisfaction, an easier life – all in return for just a few of those dollar bills.

To Walmart and its customers, price is everything. The household income of the typical Walmart shopper is slightly below the American average. One in five shopping in the store might be paying with food stamps, issued by the government to those with the lowest earnings. Walmart's pricing allows the budget of shoppers such as Lauren Miller (women outnumber men in the aisles three to one) to stretch further.

This is the American dream on the cheap. Those low prices equal big bucks for Walmart. Around $1 billion flow through its tills across America every day. Its offshoots around the globe earn a further $250 million or so. That added up to sales worth $481 billion in 2016. It's the equivalent of $900,000 every minute of every day (assuming they're open all hours). The price tags may be small but being everywhere and selling everything conceivable in large numbers pays off. And everyone needs to eat.

In the temple of low prices and endless offers, it's all too easy to slip a couple of extra items into the trolley while doing that weekly grocery shop. How about a cute $2 rubber duck for the bath? A pair of $6 headphones? A radio for under $20? It's the non-food purchases that bump up Walmart's profits. But most of those dollars aren't destined to reach Walmart's coffers, or its shareholders. Lauren Miller's new radio has only a few miles to travel to its new home but her money has many thousands more miles to travel, to a factory on the other side of the globe that churns out radios by the thousand.

Sam Walton founded Walmart, his 'pile 'em high, sell it cheap' empire, in Arkansas in 1962 under the banner ALWAYS LOW PRICES. ALWAYS. For each dollar it takes at the till, Walmart skims off about three cents in profit. So the pressure's always on to seek low costs. It's an ethos Sam maintained in every area of his life. Even after he had made his fortune, he drove a pick-up truck and shared cheap hotel rooms on business trips. Crucially, this allowed him to understand what motivated shoppers across America: the quest for a bargain. For many, that was born of desire rather than necessity. Half a century on, his strategy still has the faithful, like Lauren Miller, trekking religiously to his stores.

In Sam Walton's words, 'A lot of America-made goods simply aren't competitive, either in price, or quality, or both.' Ironically, this ultimately led to the company built by the ultra-capitalist, God-fearing Mr Walton relying heavily on an alliance with the People's Republic of China – which is where the factory that produced Lauren Miller's radio is most likely to be. Walmart disclosed it had ordered $18 billion worth of goods from China in 2004. That marked a massive jump of 40 per cent in just two years, justifying Walmart's decision to move its global sourcing headquarters to Shenzhen in 2002.

Since 2004, the company has been pretty quiet on the subject. But by counting shipping containers and poring over other data, it has been estimated that, in the decade or so since, Walmart's annual spending on Chinese-made goods has almost tripled to $50 billion. That bargain radio is a minute drop in a boundless ocean of goods reaching America's shores and shop shelves. Plants have sprung up the length of China's east coast and beyond. Ships that can transport 15,000 containers across the Pacific in just five days have been built. All to meet the insatiable appetite of Walmart shoppers. In total, China flogs as much to that one retailer – via some 20,000 suppliers – as it does to the whole of Germany or the UK. Much of every $1 spent on a toy, electrical gadget or T-shirt at a Walmart checkout in the USA is likely to end up in the coffers of a Chinese manufacturer.

Walmart is far from China's only American customer but it accounts for more than one in every ten dollars spent by the USA on Chinese-made goods. By parting with her hard-earned dollar, Lauren Miller is entering into a global contract: cheap electronics in exchange for the most important currency on earth. In 2015, goods worth almost $483 billion were shipped from China to the USA, with goods worth $116 billion going the other way. The $367 billion difference between the two – the trade gap or deficit – was the largest in history, and has swelled this century, partly due to Walmart's buying habits.

Lauren Miller is just echoing the humdrum daily routine of millions of Americans: spending a dollar at Walmart. But that humble, solitary dollar is part of an immense, global story. It is more, even, than just a cog in the thunderous machinery of the highest consuming nation on earth; it's a crucial part of the explosion in global trade that's become the economic and political story of our age, a process that's shifted not just wealth, jobs and well-being but the very centres of power too.

෴

One study estimates that Walmart has 'cost' the USA some 400,000 manufacturing jobs over the last twelve years by opting to import goods from China. Walmart denies this. What about the jobs, in distribution and logistics for example, that trade creates? And keeping shopping bills down might allow that customer to spend more money eating out or going to the cinema, boosting takings and jobs elsewhere. But it's true, they might not be the same type of jobs, or pay as well.

There's no denying that this change in employment patterns in the West has become problematic for policymakers across the developed world, and painful for workers and businesses. The irony is that the trade boom might suit Lauren Miller very well as a customer but it might be not so good for her as an American employee or business owner – in fact, it could mean no work for her at all. Back in 1985, Sam Walton's company took out full-page ads in major newspapers to announce the store's new 'Buy American' programme. As with the decision to relocate some production from the Far East to a failing Arkansas clothing factory the previous year (at the behest of Bill Clinton, then state senator), it was a move designed to appeal to Walmart's core clientele. And yet, as we know, imports from China have continued to increase.

Since the early 1990s, more than 4.5 million manufacturing jobs have disappeared in the USA. The Rust Belt – America's industrial heartland – sweeps from New York State, Pennsylvania, Ohio and Michigan, to north Indiana, Illinois and Wisconsin. As they have struggled to compete with cheaper competitors overseas, factories there have fallen silent. Flint in Michigan was the birthplace of both General Motors and filmmaker Michael Moore. Consequently, the city was the star of his documentary *Roger & Me*, which told the story of how General Motors' production took to the road. At its peak, the company employed 80,000 in Flint; now – with factories shifted elsewhere, including Mexico – that's slumped to 5,000. The population has halved to 100,000. Two out of every five of those left in Flint live in poverty. Even before a recent water-contamination scandal, the price of the average home in Flint had dropped to under $20,000.

It's an immense headache for families in towns such as Flint and their political representatives. There's huge pressure to prop up these ageing industries to enable them to compete with younger, more agile competitors from the East. Ironically, it's the very same kind of nurturing that allowed American manufacturing to thrive when it was in its infancy. Between 1816 and 1945, the USA slapped some of the highest charges anywhere in the world on the foreign goods reaching its shores. Behind that virtual wall, nascent domestic industry thrived, without the risk of being throttled by competition before the USA could emerge as a global leader.

So why wouldn't America simply choose to make everything in America, and buy only American? Being patriotic might make good political sense but it can come with a big price tag. Sam Walton chose instead to stock his shelves with goods from far away, in line with an ethos he'd also shipped in from abroad – an ethos made in Britain by the eighteenth-century economists Adam Smith and David Ricardo.

Adam Smith made his name by pondering how the humble pin was made, a process involving eighteen different stages. He argued that if a single worker were to craft each pin from start to finish, he wouldn't make many of them. However, assign each stage to a different specialist worker and the process becomes more efficient. You could make far, far more, and so earn more. If you made more than you needed to supply the local market, you could trade the excess for something else. The theory of specialisation was born.

How does this explain *what* a country chooses to specialise in, and to what extent it trades? The work of Smith and one of his followers, David Ricardo, looks at this in detail. It boils down to this: a country that trades for products that it can get more cheaply from another country is better off than if it had made the products at home. It should produce the goods it has an 'absolute advantage' in. If it can produce everything more efficiently, it may still benefit from focusing on the goods it's relatively best at – what it has a 'comparative advantage' in.

It hinges on how much it costs to produce something in a particular place. What influences those costs? Many factors are at play: the availability of natural resources, climate, land, size of workforce, wages, rent, regulations, skills, machinery and transport. China has a plentiful, young workforce and relatively few regulations. For every dollar a company has to spend employing a Chinese factory worker, it would have to fork out roughly five times as much for an equivalent American worker. Walmart can source goods more cheaply in China because the Chinese have become specialists in low-tech manufacturing. Plants in Shenzhen can churn out toys and electronics at a fraction of the cost of a factory in Michigan. For the Chinese manufacturer – and everyone else – selling goods to the USA is a no-brainer. American consumers account for one in every five dollars spent around the globe; it's still the largest market in the world.

But the traffic is not all in one direction. Years of specialist cultivation, a temperate climate and the right kind of soil mean that the USA has been able to carve out a niche in the production of soybeans, something that China, blighted by soil erosion and an erratic water supply, has failed to do. America accounts for one-third of the world's output of soy, which is used in cooking products and animal feed. Naturally, its biggest customer is the world's most populous country. As China gets richer, so does its appetite for meat, and therefore for livestock feed. Two out of every three soybeans produced in the USA reach Chinese shores, and those imports have tripled in the last decade.

At the other end of the spectrum, the USA dominates in the sale of high-spec, high-tech machinery and equipment. For example, China bought $8 billion worth of aircraft from America last year. US aerospace giant Boeing excitedly forecast that China could order over $1 trillion worth of planes in the next twenty years, and it envisages retaining the lion's share of the market.

Why does China not plan to invest more in its own aerospace industry, and America focus more on the needs of its own people?

Imagine if all the factory workers in the USA and China made either aircraft or radios. Let's assume these are very adept workforces, there are minimal transport costs and no trading obstacles, such as tariffs. For every aeroplane China produces, let's say it could make 100,000 radios. And that for every two planes the USA produces, it could make 100,000 radios. If both countries decided to make both radios and planes, in the same period of time they could produce in total three planes and 200,000 radios.

What if both countries specialised in making planes? The USA would make the smaller sacrifice, forgoing fewer radios (50,000) than China (100,000) to make each extra plane. So the USA might decide to leave radio production to China and focus all its attention on planes, and vice versa. In that case, we would end up with four planes from the USA, and 200,000 radios from China. Using the same resources across the two countries, the end result is greater overall.

What if China could manufacture *everything*, including planes (which it can't at the moment), more cheaply and efficiently in the future? It would still make sense for the USA to specialise in the production of aircraft if it can make them more efficiently (compared to radios) than China can. Imagine if, for example, with the same resources the USA can make two planes *or* 50,000 radios, while China could make three planes *or* 150,000 radios. The USA has to sacrifice 25,000 radios for each plane it makes, while China has to forego 50,000. That sacrifice is the way economists measure the 'cost' of making that plane. The USA sacrifices less, which means it has a comparative advantage in making planes. And if they each specialise, the end result is still greater overall.

So specialisation and free trade mean more goods and lower costs. And lower costs mean lower price tags. China has the planes it needs to satisfy the wanderlust of its increasingly prosperous population and Lauren Miller saves money by buying a Chinese radio at Walmart. As a consequence she has more to spend on other items, such as taking her kids to the bowling alley at the weekend.

Lower prices mean a lower cost of living. As inflation equals the rate at which the cost of living rises, there's less of that too.

Keeping a lid on inflation, thus ensuring economic and financial stability, is the main task of the central banks, which are responsible for managing the money supply, interest rates and hence overall economies of their respective countries. They have a target rate of inflation. If prices are rising faster than this, the banks normally raise interest rates, to deter borrowing and reduce spending, making it harder for retailers to raise prices. Those Chinese low-priced goods help to keep the US interest rates low too, and that in turn keeps the cost of borrowing down for households and businesses. Cheap Chinese imports help Lauren Miller afford the mortgage on her home and the things she wants to put in it.

In short, free trade promises a higher standard of living all round. Or does it?

The reality is that the world doesn't work like the one described above, nor has it ever done. For a start, transport, even in the age of containerisation, does have a cost, both financial and environmental. It's one reason why China's domestic car production is growing all the time, and is greater than that of the USA and Japan combined.

Also, workers simply aren't that versatile. Someone adept at assembling radios might not be equipped to design an aircraft. The skills are very different and are not easily acquired, which can spell mass job losses that can be catastrophic for towns such as Flint. Forking out on a new Chinese-made radio might seem to be a decision that makes financial sense on a personal level, but on a national scale, the political and economic implications are enormous.

Lauren Miller's weekly visit to Walmart is repeated in countries around the globe. The dollars, euros, yen and other currencies those shoppers spend have fired up prosperity in developing countries by making them the workshops of the world. Giant retailers such as Walmart now sell cheap radios to communities in the Rust Belt, communities that once made such goods themselves. Now that those industries have been priced out of existence, the people who once worked in them may find themselves more dependent on low-cost retailers such as Walmart to make ends meet. And, ironically, this is due partly to Walmart's preference for chasing bargains in other countries. Those who argue that it's the factory workers in the West who have paid the price for cheaper goods have become ever more vocal.

In theory, globalisation and free trade are in the interest of consumers and countries *as a whole*. In theory. But the citizens of Guangzhou or Tijuana don't have a vote in American elections. Those who've lost their livelihoods in Flint do. What's good for the world at large – or even America as a whole, if it benefits from a lower cost of living – isn't necessarily good for the neighbourhood economy, or for the statesmen and women who are accountable to its residents. Some, not just in America, feel the rewards of globalisation have passed them by. Because of the outcry from the 'losers' in the game, the tide is turning back towards nationalism and isolation – or, rather, smaller trade pacts with your nearest and/ or dearest, rather than a free (trade) for all. Domestic politics and the global economy are on a collision course.

What can governments do to protect failing industries or regions against the perils of free trade – maybe even reduce that trade gap? They can limit our choices, for a start. They can make that Chinese radio less attractive, or make it disappear altogether. Want people to buy American? Then make imports relatively expensive or hard to get hold of. Try slapping a tariff on things entering the country, or enforce a quota on the amount allowed in.

In fact, truly free trade rarely exists. From customs officers checking suitcases for contraband to the surcharges that double the price of goods entering Bhutan, there are barriers to commerce everywhere. They take many forms.

On occasion, countries even impose a charge on goods *leaving* their shores, making them more expensive for overseas buyers. That might sound strange when usually the battle's on to undercut your neighbour; it's even stranger when the perpetrator is China. But, at one time, it did just that. High international grain prices were tempting Chinese farmers to sell abroad, leading to a domestic shortage. To shift the balance, the government effectively taxed exports, such was its concern about feeding its own people. China has one-fifth of the world's population but only 7 per cent of its arable land.

Equally, a government could slip a failing industry some cash via a direct subsidy – as has happened with some European airlines – or by cutting its tax bill. Even more bluntly, a country can try to control its exchange rate. The lower the value of its currency, the cheaper and more alluring its exports. It's something China has been accused of repeatedly.

The steel industry provides a fascinating example of all this. Steel is currently making headlines internationally. China's meteoric rise to become the world's factory – and a decision to build its way out of the 2008 global financial crisis – meant a boom in construction, which prompted a huge appetite for steel. By 2015, China was producing half of the world's steel, with most of it destined for domestic use. The government subsidised both the energy used in the manufacture of steel and the steel producers themselves. That meant China could sell the stuff for less than it should cost to manufacture anywhere in the world: a process that goes by the inelegant term of 'dumping'. It drove down the price of steel around the globe.

Established steel producers struggled to stay in business while crying foul. Then China's construction boom eased off, leading to a glut of steel. China offloaded more onto the world market and the price fell even further. Elsewhere, steelmakers were forced to throw in the towel, closing plants and cutting jobs. In 2016, steel production in the USA was roughly half the level seen in 1973.

The implications of the collapse of the steel industry spread way beyond the Rust Belt. For a country to safeguard its security, it needs to ensure that it can go it alone in producing food, water and weapons, and maybe even steel. These industries are often dubbed 'strategic'. Shielding them is important. Some nations even claim steel is a strategic industry.

There are several ways that the USA (or any other country) can protect its industries, and at the same time reap additional benefits. Most of these centre on restricting the price or quantities of goods coming in, or finding a way to engineer an increase in the amount it can flog abroad. When this happens, importing becomes unattractive and retailers will look closer to home for supplies. Struggling manufacturers might fire up some factories again, protecting or even creating jobs. And tariffs spell extra cash for the government. This is good news for both household budgets in Michigan and the government's budget. It is less so for factories in Shenzhen.

The obvious reaction would be for China to hit back with its own tariffs and trade barriers against US-made goods. That kind of retaliation quickly escalates into a trade war. The result? It's not just the factory in Shenzhen that loses business; it's also Boeing and Ford, as China opts for planes built by Europe's Airbus and cars made by VW. Other jobs and entire businesses could be at risk.

Alternatively, some workers might find their jobs protected by policies that keep imports at bay. However, they'll pay the price when they spend their wages, as tariffs mean imports becoming more expensive. A higher cost of living tends to prompt the central bank to raise interest rates. Not only would shoppers' money not go as far, it's likely they'd have less choice as some imports would disappear. So much for a higher standard of living.

Production processes are complex. An 'American' Boeing plane can contain engines from the UK, Canadian navigation radios, and titanium from China. Put up the duties on Chinese imports and Boeing feels the pinch. The typical iPhone contains components from at least a dozen countries, including Taiwan, China and Germany. If Washington clamps down on free trade, Apple's customers and investors in Silicon Valley feel the burn.

To what extent would cutting imports from China allow America to reboot manufacturing? Employment in the manufacturing sector had actually gone into decline *before* the USA signed free-trade agreements with, for example, Mexico. Technology probably played as much of a role as factories thousands of miles away in making US jobs obsolete. Slapping on tariffs might not make much of a difference. The robots are already here.

The impact of a trade war could be massive. In 2016, America's incoming President Trump mooted a 45 per cent tariff on Chinese goods. Economists at banks such as HSBC and Daiwa Capital Markets estimated that as a consequence exports to the USA might drop by between 50 and 85 per cent – or by up to $420 billion. That could dent China's income by as much as 5 per cent, threatening millions of jobs.

For a stark example of the impact of trade barriers, take a look at America's Great Depression. In the 1920s, the economy had enjoyed a spectacular boom: spending, production and investment in the stock market grew too far, too fast. It couldn't last. Shares on Wall Street lost one-third of their value in a week in the stock market crash of 1929, hitting consumer confidence, wealth and spending. Companies laid off workers by the thousand. What should have been a relatively brief recession, a reversal in the economy's fortunes, was exacerbated when the authorities initially failed to pump more money in (so-called 'quantitative easing') to shore up the financial system. Then came the 1930 Smoot–Hawley Act. That hiked up tariffs on 890 agricultural imports. Its aim was to prop up American farmers, whose businesses had been ravaged by the unprecedented series of severe dust storms and droughts across the prairies of Canada and the USA known as the Dust Bowl. Instead, impoverished Americans faced soaring food prices. Other countries reacted with their own tariffs, and world trade dropped by 65 per cent. The same kind of protectionism that had allowed the USA to build up its industries a century earlier was now deepening the pain of the Great Depression.

Carrying the scars not only of this trade war but also of the Second World War, the USA invited its battlefield allies to discuss an agreement to cut tariffs on trade in goods. The World Bank and the International Monetary Fund (IMF) had just been created in order to coordinate financial policy; the idea was to have an equivalent to facilitate trade.

In 1947, under the unwieldy title of the General Agreement on Tariffs and Trade (GATT), discussions in Geneva succeeded in starting to chip away at those barriers. Some 45,000 trade concessions

~en twenty-three countries, affecting $10 billion
. Not bad for seven months' work.

at was just the start. Most trade barriers remained, and the concessions that had been won focused on reducing not eliminating tariffs. Over the next half a century or so, the talks continued, aiming to set rules to free up world trade. In 1995, GATT gave birth to the World Trade Organization (WTO). It was more than just a change of logo. While GATT's purpose was to create a rulebook for trade, the WTO is the body that manages and promotes freer trade by building on the rules already set, and policing them. It ensures those rules are followed. Membership is voluntary and has climbed steadily. In 2001, its 143rd member was China.

The WTO now has over 160 members. The big boys get most of the headlines, but over three-quarters of WTO members are lower-income countries, often trying to get their industries off the ground. Cutting them a deal on trade barriers is allowed. In fact, the WTO has prioritised helping developing countries to advance.

A huge part of the WTO's role is settling disputes, and in the world's largest legislative and judicial body, decisions are made by consensus. Should China be allowed to subsidise rice production? Is it fair for government money to be used to bail out the American car industry after the 2008 financial crisis? The WTO must sift through evidence of the 'he said, she said' sort as if it is arbitrating playground fights. About five hundred complaints were brought to the WTO in the first twenty years of its life.

Most of those complaints centre on dumping – goods being sold for less than they cost to produce, as with Chinese steel, usually thanks to a government bailout. It's impossible to compete with goods at such low prices, but on the other hand, cheaper steel, for example, has benefited manufacturing and construction projects around the globe. However, if a country is deemed to have broken the rules, the WTO might allow retaliation. The EU and the USA have been able to slap charges on some of those cheap Chinese steel imports.

On the whole, the WTO has resulted in freer – although not free – trade. And since trade means economies generally grow faster, that's resulted in more jobs and higher incomes as well as greater choice and lower prices for consumers.

Lauren Miller's decision to purchase a radio at Walmart's checkout will be the start of a lengthy journey for her dollar. That journey offers a glimpse of just how closely the USA's prosperity is linked to its trade with the rest of the world. The quest for a better standard of living means customers are always on the prowl for cheaper goods. To stop Lauren Miller heading to Kmart or Target, Walmart has to make sure its prices remain low – preferably, lower than its competitors'. That means sourcing stock from the cheapest available supplier, wherever they happen to be in the world, providing a flow of dollars into their businesses' pockets.

How can China, and other countries, undercut the USA this way? Why are wages in Shenzhen a fraction of those in the USA? How does Walmart get away with paying $13 per hour to a checkout operator in Texas but less than $2 per hour to someone doing the same job in their Chinese stores?

Much of the discrepancy is down to demographics. There are over 900 million Chinese of working age, five times the equivalent number in the USA. And, on average, they're younger than their American counterparts. If you want to staff a factory or superstore in China, you can have your pick of workers, and you won't have to pay as much to lure them in.

For Chinese workers, the alternative to taking up that factory job is less appealing. Traditionally, countries advance from being largely agricultural towards manufacturing and then on to an economy that is more services based. China is at a relatively early stage of this process. For many of those working to make toys for Walmart, the choice in the last few decades has been between toiling on a farm or heading for the relatively more lucrative spoils of the Pearl River Delta. Wages are higher on the assembly line partly as a wider range of skills is required.

Even now, manufacturing in China and America are very different. The USA still excels in high-tech industries involving advanced design: planes rather than light bulbs. This requires more specialised equipment and highly qualified workers, which tends to result in the workforce being more productive. Partly this is because the USA has a head start; it had its industrial revolution 140 years ago.

China woke up to the idea of becoming the world's workshop only a few decades ago. For a century and a half, the USA has had a business environment more conducive to new ideas and competition. In China, Confucian culture and the legacy of communism neither promoted the concept of innovation nor provided the framework to foster entrepreneurship. Private ownership of land, for example, was permitted only in 1978. From the free exchange of information to the tax system to the protection of intellectual property, China has been slow off the mark to encourage and protect pioneering ideas. Until very recently, the focus has tended to be on following central business plans rather than nurturing start-ups. The USA topped the table as the best place to be an entrepreneur in 2015. China limped in at 61. Pioneering ideas tend to result in more productive employees, who then attract a higher wage.

But while America might give the likes of Steve Jobs more freedom to develop their ideas, it also places far more restrictions on them in one area: the protection of their employees. From health and safety in the workplace to the numbers of hours worked, the rules are far tougher in America. In China, a blind eye might still be turned to the use of child labour, the application of a minimum wage or even observation of environmental law. Workplace injuries are far more common than in the West.

Partly in response to customer outrage, global companies such as Walmart have stepped up scrutiny of their Chinese suppliers. But when there are 80,000 factories supplying retailers from thousands of miles away, keeping an eye on them all the time is a challenge. Human rights organisations claim the more unscrupulous bosses are adept at circumventing checks.

The consequences can be horrific, and not only for the workforce: 173 people lost their lives in two massive explosions in Tianjin after hazardous chemicals were stored unsafely in a warehouse dangerously close to housing; 120 died in a fire in a poultry-processing factory, due to treacherous conditions and locked fire escapes. These are only two examples from dozens of major industrial accidents in China in recent years.

Smaller-scale accidents affecting the livelihoods of individual workers are common. There is no culture of compensation, no expectation that the employer should meet the costs of medical care. Workers can be easily replaced. For employers, life can be as cheap as labour. It can be argued that some workers in China are paying a deadly price for globalisation while being unable to afford its spoils.

The breathless anticipation that greets the unveiling of every new version of the iPhone bears out how Apple's handset has become an international lifestyle icon. Those launches may happen in Silicon Valley but the handsets themselves are assembled thousands of miles of away, mainly in Zhengzhou in China, at the plants of a company called Foxconn. In 2017, the newest model could cost as much as $999. That's about a month's pay for someone on the assembly line. But it would take the average American in Lauren Miller's neighbourhood less than half that time to earn the money to pay for it.

To first-world hipsters, the price tag on the iPhone is reassuringly high. Some estimates put the actual cost of assembling each handset at about $30. Even accounting for Apple's research and design costs, we don't need the brain of Steve Jobs to work out that the profit margin is colossal. The iPhone is out of reach of the Foxconn employees who painstakingly put them together. But then it isn't aimed at Foxconn workers. Apple knows that better-off customers around the world are willing to fork out for the prestige of owning one, and it sets its prices accordingly.

Apple produces a slightly cheaper handset for lower-income countries. In China, this model has failed to beat cheaper brands. That the country is, however, one of Apple's core markets reveals a thirst for the top-of-the range models and an ability to pay for them among China's wealthy elite. Globalisation has imported a particular Western feature to post-communist China: inequality of income. The gulf between richest and poorest is on the same scale as it is in America.

On the whole, the cost of living in China is not as high as it is in the USA. The price of the goods and services, from clothing to housing, that people actually spend their money on is lower

– unless we're talking imported smartphones, for example. (That's on average: obviously, compare the glitzy high-rise financial districts in Shanghai and the suburbs of Indianapolis and you'd get a different answer. But they're exceptions.) Generally, Chinese wages don't go as far in China as American ones do in the USA, so Chinese workers see a lower standard of living than their American counterparts. Add in pollution and a lack of individual freedoms and the Chinese quality of life is lower. But that may change.

China has been transformed beyond recognition in the last fifty years or so. The middle of the last century saw industrialisation on a massive scale, under stringent government control. Then, in the 1970s, restrictions were lifted on how much businesses could produce and who could buy their goods. Companies could keep their profits and set their own wages. Most importantly, they could sell abroad. The way was set for China to become the world's factory. Between 1978 and 2012, China's economy grew by nearly 10 per cent per year, according to official statistics. Scepticism reigns about how reliable those numbers are but they do suggest growth several times the American average.

As people flocked from rural areas to the factories, their income increased. Since 1978, over 700 million people have been taken out of poverty. A study from consultants McKinsey & Company estimates that the Chinese middle class has grown rapidly from a mere 5 million in 2000 to 225 million, and is set to rise further. These new middle classes typically earn between $11,000 and $43,000, own property and live in urban areas. So close to the American dream and yet so very different.

Where next for China? With liberalisation and prosperity come demands as well as aspirations, despite the constraints of the communist government. Low wages might have been the key to China's export success, but the workers have started to push back. Increasingly aware of their worth, they've been demanding improvements in wages, hours and working conditions. So why not simply replace these workers with less troublesome staff? It's no longer that easy. The likes of Foxconn and Walmart's suppliers have to dig deeper and deeper into rural areas to fill vacancies.

This is partly the result of government action. In 1979, a 'one-child policy' was introduced that was to last for thirty-five years. This succeeded in curbing the high birth rate but has also had disturbing consequences. A preference for boys resulted in female infanticide and abortion. Men now outnumber women by over 60 million. And the average age of the population has rapidly increased: by 2050, one in four Chinese will be over sixty-five. China's workforce is actually shrinking.

Whereas typical new recruits to the factory floor used to be in their teens or early twenties, now they may be in their forties. While China might fall short of international labour laws, workers have now started to fashion their own system of industrial relations. The growing awareness of – and opposition to – sweatshop conditions from shoppers around the globe has also piled the pressure on employers.

As a result, earnings have shot up. Across China, wages jumped 9.5 per cent in 2014, the slowest growth in earned income since 2000. It's the kind of pay rise most of those in the West, although their pay cheques remain several times higher, can only dream of. Recently, that upward trend in earned income has sat quite well with the Chinese government's plans, which are published every five years. The administration wants growth to be driven more by domestic consumers, and that can happen only if they have cash in their pockets.

However, a higher wage bill pushes up production costs, putting Chinese factories under pressure. Rather than charge Walmart more and risk losing the contract, businesses have been pulling out all the stops to keep costs down. Investing in better technology to speed up manufacturing and raise productivity is one option. Or, given that China is a massive, diverse country, why not relocate to where workers are cheaper, rather than sit in Shenzhen and wait for them to come to you? Foxconn, for example, is now building phones in Henan, Sichuan and Guiyang provinces, where wages are much lower, land is cheaper and there are more tax breaks to be enjoyed. It's only a temporary solution, though. Ultimately, costs in these regions will rise too, and sooner or later the factories will have to hike their prices.

Faced with a bigger bill, how will Walmart respond? It could take a hit on its profits and carry on ordering. But that would upset its shareholders. Or it could raise in-store prices accordingly. That could upset the customers, who might then head for the aisles of Target or Kmart instead, although these retailers are likely to be facing the same issues.

Or Walmart could take its business elsewhere. Is this an opportunity to buy American? Possibly, but, as we've seen, that would still cost several times as much. How about shopping around a bit further afield? Lauren Miller's spending power is up for grabs to the best – in this case the lowest – bidder. This is where the likes of Vietnam and the Philippines come in.

Wages in Vietnam make China's look almost munificent. The minimum wage for a textile worker in Vietnam is about $100 per month. That's less than one-fifth of the amount a worker in China would earn for stitching together the same T-shirt.

'Made in Vietnam' labels are now common in clothing sold by the biggest global names on the high street, from H&M to Uniqlo, and hanging in Lauren Miller's family's wardrobe. Walmart set up a sourcing office in Ho Chi Minh City in 2013. The garment and textile industry now makes up $3 of every $20 earned across the Vietnamese economy, and employs almost 3.5 million people.

Vietnam has been held back by its need to import most of the materials – from fabric to zips – needed by its relatively small companies and less sophisticated distribution systems. But the government has ambitious plans to change that, including a new airport and a trade deal with the EU. The textiles industry has its eye on doubling export earnings within the next decade.

Those plans will have suffered a setback when the USA backed out of a trade deal involving Vietnam. That deal – the Trans-Pacific Partnership (TPP) – would have sliced the tariffs (on average 17 per cent) that the USA currently puts on textile imports from Vietnam. Nevertheless, the country will continue to snap at China's heels; its factories are an increasingly attractive alternative.

In time, wages in Vietnam too will rise. Then what? The world's retailers will seek out the next bargain-basement supplier. Bangladesh and Cambodia are cheaper. However, lack of regulations and appropriate procedures, which led to disasters such as the tragic collapse of the Rana Plaza factory in Dhaka, which killed over 1,100 people, makes them a less attractive prospect. That could change. Then there's Myanmar, where H&M is now sourcing jumpers. It's an increasingly dynamic and competitive picture. Many other countries are joining in the battle for Lauren Miller's dollar.

Where does that leave China? Having established a firm foothold and reputation, it seems destined to remain the key manufacturer of simple goods for some time. But the evolution of its homegrown brands such as phone maker Xiaomi prove China is carving its own niche in high-tech design as well as in production.

It's no longer leaving it to the USA. The explosion of a middle class with shopping habits to match has created a wealth of opportunities and, for example, propelled the growth of e-commerce giant Alibaba, which burst on to the global stage with the biggest launch ever seen on the USA stock market. In 2016, it overtook Walmart as the largest retailer on the planet, only with largely virtual aisles instead of real ones.

For the moment, though, back to the more traditional bricks-and-mortar way of retailing in those Walmart stores. There, China remains the primary source of the multitude of affordable goods piled high on the shelves. The dollar Lauren Miller parted company with at the Walmart checkout in Texas is passed on to a radio manufacturer 8,000 miles away in Shenzhen. However, it won't hang on to that dollar for long.

2

Making – and working
– the global red carpet

China

Ever heard of No. 32 Chengfang Street, Beijing? It's hardly as well known as Buckingham Palace, the White House or the Kremlin. But it should be. It's the site of almost unrivalled economic power, affecting the fortunes of those not just in China and across Asia, but even on the other side of the globe – including Lauren Miller.

To find Chengfang Street, you have to head inside Beijing's Second Ring Road (there are four in total) towards the glass and steel of Beijing Financial Street: this is China's Wall Street, completed in time for the 2008 Olympics, where you'll find banks and regulators jostling for space. For all their familiar Western, corporate exteriors, the towers are based around internal courtyards, similar to those in the ancient hutong neighbourhoods that surround the Forbidden City. However, there's nothing ancient about what goes on here. China's stock exchange may be in Shanghai but the thirty-five blocks that form Beijing Financial Street are the biggest monetary and financial market in the country. Trillions of renminbi, as the Chinese currency is known, pass through here every day.

At its heart is No. 32 Chengfang Street, better known as the People's Bank of China. The country's central bank has resided in Beijing since its creation in 1949, in this relatively small and increasingly cramped horseshoe-shaped building. At a modest nine storeys, No. 32 is dwarfed by its more modern, glitzier, sky-scraping neighbours, but its appearance is deceptive. From this low-key base the bank influences the economic fates of billions of people around the world.

It's into this opaque system, still with an element of state own-ership or control lingering on, that our dollar will find a path. After it was founded in 1949, the People's Bank of China was the only bank, central or commercial, in the country for nearly three decades. It has since been broken up into separate banks: a mas-sive economy that was opening up to the world was too much for a single bank to deal with, even with regional offices. Chengfang Street was in danger of overload, a victim of its own success. In the 1980s, the commercial banking arm of the People's Bank of China was split off into four independent but state-owned special-ist banks: these big four are the Industrial and Commercial Bank of China (ICBC), China Construction Bank (CCB), Bank of China (BOC) and Agricultural Bank of China (ABC).

Lauren Miller's dollar has winged its way to the Shenzhen-based electronics company Mingtian. Its roaring factory is jostling alongside thousands of others, competing to survive and thrive. Shenzhen isn't just China's manufacturing heartland; it's emerg-ing as its Silicon Valley, where innovation and brainwaves meet production. To be part of that, Mingtian doesn't need dollars. It needs renminbi – or, as the Chinese currency is also called, yuan – in order to pay its workers and buy components at the ten-storey Huaqiangbe electronics market, the largest in China. It can then invest in developing in new products, such as drones and cameras. And it can stay one step ahead of the *shanzhai*, the fakes that are produced just as fast but more cheaply than the real thing.

When Mingtian's finance official presents Lauren Miller's dollar to a commercial bank in exchange for local currency – either as notes, or in the company's own bank balance – where does it end up? The central bank ultimately keeps a close grip on currency entering the country: our dollar works its way back up the banking food chain and arrives in the coffers of the People's Bank of China. It won't be lonely.

It might be a relatively new player in the globalisation game but China has embraced the dollar tightly to afford it immense power both at home and abroad. The country's economic progress over the last seventy years has shocked the world, and is likely to continue to do so. In recent years, China has achieved its success on the world stage partly by diverting attention away from its competitors. As its economic star has ascended, there's been a mighty power struggle in the region.

Japan had seized Asia's limelight in the second half of the twentieth century, producing familiar household names such as Sony and Toyota, and becoming the go-to player for high-tech gadgetry. But stars can fade as quickly as they rise. In Japan's case, the hype and confidence in the economy caused it to inflate too far. In the early 1990s, reality hit: the stock market slumped and the economy followed. A little of the pain filtered as far as South Korea and Taiwan. What followed for Japan was a 'lost decade': weak growth and few jobs created. This coincided with China becoming the hottest thing in town.

However, Japan remains on the A-list. Its economy is still one of the world's three largest and it's beginning to prosper again. Japan may get fewer headlines – and less notoriety – but in Asia it jostles subtly for top billing with China. They make an uneasy double act, relying heavily on each other for regional custom and success. Traditionally, China has produced basic components, which Japan uses to assemble sophisticated gadgets. Meanwhile, Japan is producing the sophisticated components China needs to assemble products – including phone handsets. And the two are reliant on each other's consumers for custom. Given China's own high-tech aspirations, Japan could find its star yet further eclipsed.

As we saw in the last chapter, reeling in Lauren Miller's dollar is partly about creating income and jobs for China and for the radio manufacturer, Mingtian. But that isn't the whole story. The trading relationship between China and the USA is about *money* – and not just for its own sake. It's part of China's battle to take centre stage.

Who is producing China's economic blockbuster? Meet Zhou Xiaochuan. He's been chairman of the People's Bank of China since 2002. A chemical engineer by training, Zhou Xiaochuan might seem an unlikely chief central banker. He started his career in farming before moving on to academia to cultivate plans to reform the Chinese economy. As the country's head banker, by 2017 he'd outlasted three Chinese presidents and countless rivals around the globe. What is the secret to his survival? He is renowned as a moderniser, the man who's successfully steered China and its currency to stellar heights. China is constantly facing uncharted territory and – despite some missteps – Zhou has won himself a reputation as the man to steer the complex economy.

It's a position of immense power, but Zhou's wife, Li Ling, is likely to ensure his feet are still on the ground. Until recently, she was a senior figure in the Department of Commerce, responsible for trade deals and disputes. It was up to her to figure out how to keep China's goods flowing west, even when the US economy and political will retreated.

Li Ling's efforts on the trade front paved the way for Chinese factories to sell to Walmart and secure the custom and dollars of Americans including Lauren Miller. Meanwhile, her husband has enabled these manufacturers to become established and to grow to meet that demand, making it easier for firms in Shenzhen to bank their earnings, and exchange them from dollars to renminbi to pay their bills. Trade and the evolution of China's financial system are inextricably linked.

Since 1949, China has burst from the shadows to vie for space alongside the star of the show: the USA and its mighty dollar. It wants main billing, on its own terms. But, for that, it needs the USA to remain a major player. It is harnessing dollars and turning them as a weapon against their creator, the USA. It's a war of currencies, in which the dollar is the key weapon at the heart of a complex plot.

China, like any prospering business, has a lot of money coming in. Over the years that it's been selling radios and other goods to the USA (and to the rest of the world), its stash has rapidly built up. A massive amount of cash has flowed into the People's Bank of China. Because those earnings are primarily driven by selling exports, they're are known as 'foreign reserves'. China (and other countries) will often hold this money in foreign currency, typically dollars or yen, or gold – or indeed anything that can quickly be converted into cash. It's used for trade, or, in an emergency, to rescue the economy. In China, the make-up and location of these reserves are a state secret. Lauren Miller's dollar will almost certainly be held electronically, but the reserves held in gold could be destined for a vault in Beijing, or they could fall under the careful eye of the army.

Wherever those greenbacks are being held, what's certain is that Chengfang Street has clutched them to its heart and used them to build its power base. China has become wealthy by exporting cheap goods, but that price advantage is not just about the low cost of assembling radios. It's also about the price of Chinese *currency*.

When that dollar was exchanged at the bank, it was just one of billions coming into China from the USA, much more money than is going in the opposite direction. By demanding that businesses deposit those dollars, the central bank effectively becomes the owner of all dollars in China. In practice, the likes of Mingtian have to buy their own currency from the bank with the dollars they've earned, exchanging one currency for another.

An exchange rate is simply the price of one currency expressed in another currency. With all those dollars looking for yuan, the yuan should become more expensive. It's supply and demand: if there are only a certain number of yuan, and everyone wants them, people will have to hand over more dollars for their yuan.

Those stripy-shirted dealers snapping into phones on trading floors aren't just a well-worn cliché of films about Wall Street. They're a regular presence in currency dealing rooms across the globe. These men and, increasingly, women are setting exchange rates, matching the supply of and demand for different currencies to arrive at the right price. If there are more people looking to buy dollars than are selling them, the price goes up. If China's exporting more to America, the demand for yuan goes up, and China's exchange rate should rise.

That's how it works in theory, but because all dollars have to be traded via the central bank, it can set their price. For many years, the price of the dollar was set artificially high and the price of the yuan artificially low. (Fewer dollars were required to buy yuan; equally, to buy dollars, say for use in trade, a Chinese business had to shell out more yuan than might otherwise be the case.) The bank achieved this by doling out more yuan per dollar than perhaps was reasonable.

One of the responsibilities of a central bank is to ensure that there's enough money around to keep an economy going. It issues the bills and coins, the fuel that keeps the wheels of prosperity turning. It ensures enough money is printed to exchange for dollars at the price – the exchange rate – that it prefers. (This is a risky business. Push too much money into an economy too fast, and there's too much cash chasing too few goods. Demand is ramped up, and so is the rate at which prices rise, which means higher inflation. The bank avoids this by trying to influence the money supply through some technical tinkering known as 'sterilisation'. That's where it sells bonds to the public in order to mop up excess cash.)

A freely moving exchange rate, known as a 'floating' rate, is common across much of the world. Floating currencies can be legally traded in foreign exchange markets, where their values are determined. China, however, is different. The People's Bank of China has kept a grip on the exchange rate by regulating its trade and other policies. While it went all out to promote its exporting power, for many years it forcibly kept the yuan down, at a of its true value. What is the advantage of keeping the currency down? Surely a strong exchange rate is a thing of beauty; a sign of power and might that will see off all comers on the global stage; a sign of confidence in the economy. Why wouldn't China want to take the almighty dollar's crown and complete its superpower image?

As China's export boom took off, a higher exchange rate would have made China's exports appear more expensive. It would suddenly cost more dollars to buy that radio. Its price in yuan might not have changed, but its price in dollars would have. This would make China's products a lot less attractive to American buyers. Even a couple of dollars more on a price tag could have made Lauren Miller put her radio back on the shelf. She might find that buying American is actually not that different, price wise. Or how about a radio made in South Korea or Japan instead? That would be a blow to the Chinese manufacturer, and a loss for China too.

Flogging stuff to the rest of the world has been China's ticket to becoming one of the most prosperous economies around, effectively transferring income from Lauren Miller to its shores. The central bank worked hard to keep the yuan down and exports irresistibly cheap to Walmart's shoppers. A lower exchange rate equals cheaper exports. (It also makes imports dearer, convincing the Chinese they're better off buying Chinese.) By contrast, a stronger dollar can lead to weaker growth for the USA, as it disadvantages its exporters by making their products more expensive.

The advantage of controlling a currency's value like this is that, as well as maybe stealing a competitive edge, it promises certainty and, to a degree, stability. Businesses and consumers know what prices in shops are likely to be. They're more likely to invest and spend knowing with some confidence what the future looks like.

China has an additional interest in keeping the value of the dollar up (and, ideally, rising): it boosts the value of those reserves it's carefully accumulated from exporting. That makes China – or rather, its government – wealthier (as few of its people will ever see that wealth).

If China's management of its currency has made it the star turn, why aren't its competitors following suit? It's not that many haven't tried (and about half of the countries in the world still do, to some extent). Control comes at a price, for the central bank and for households. If a currency is very low, exports may be cheaper, but imports, goods brought in from abroad, are much, much more expensive. In a country that has to import much of its food, that can be crippling. A weaker currency can be good for business but bad for households.

It may be that a fixed currency is seen as being too strong. China doesn't have to look too far from its borders to remember a painful, expensive example. In the 1990s, many other Asian economies were making waves on the global stage. Thailand, Korea and Indonesia were among those known as the tigers: the next big things. Their export booms were causing their economies to roar. Investors were pouring in cash to grab a slice of that gold rush, shoring up demand for the Thai baht. But then they started to doubt the strength of the Thai economy and that massive wave of gloom prompted them to pull out. That meant a drop in demand for the baht, whose value was tightly managed against the dollar. When that happens, a central bank usually pours in its own money to boost the demand and keep the price of the currency up. The Thai government and its allies simply couldn't pour in money fast enough to keep the baht from falling. That caused shockwaves in currency and stock markets across the region and a full-blown Asian financial crisis. The domino effect had an impact on the other tigers, even causing tremors in Japan. Trying to maintain a fixed exchange rate can be a costly business, and cause problems throughout the economy.

Many countries have decided it's easier to let its currency do its own thing and float freely, which can actually be helpful to the economy overall. If demand for American exports falls sharply, demand for the dollar does too, and the exchange rate falls. So those exports become more attractively priced, stoking up demand again. Flexible exchange rates are a kind of automatic shock absorber for trade. (That's the theory, anyway. For it to work in practice, the demand for exports/imports has to be responsive to changes in price. And it isn't always.)

The countries that play by those rules, allowing their exchange rates to fluctuate, see the likes of China as playing foul. Politicians argued for many years that by keeping down its exchange rate China was keeping the price of its exports artificially low. There's no way an American manufacturer could compete with Mingtian for Lauren Miller's custom.

China's central bank was seen as exerting extreme control to promote its own wares, and its actions have led to lurid headlines across the globe. A fixed currency can have a political price. China's been accused of being a 'manipulator' which 'doesn't play fair on trade'. That's not just tabloid sensationalism. Senior politicians, all the way up to the US president, have claimed the Asian giant is 'cheating', waging an 'all-out currency war' designed to 'cripple' America. It might sound like a petulant playground squabble but there's some immensely serious business at stake here.

It's not just the USA but other Asian manufacturing nations who have felt their exporters have been disadvantaged by China's actions. Many countries, including Japan, have fiddled their own exchange rates over the years, but China's performance has been the most dramatic. The Americans have blamed China for stealing business by stealth, by undercutting their producers and enabling that almighty trade deficit. As those complaints have grown louder, China's hold on the exchange rate has finally loosened. But only a little. The value of the yuan still hovers between 6.5 and 7 to the dollar, pretty much as it did a decade ago. Mingtian still enjoys a competitive edge.

Over the years, the Chinese government's obsessive control over its currency has meant that it has clung tightly to those trillions of dollars earned along the way. But those dollars haven't been stashed under a giant mattress in the basement of Chengfang Street. They've been used to invest in China's future.

What would we buy if money were no object? If it was just a few million, then Lauren Miller or the owner of Mingtian might dream of holiday homes, even an island in the tropics, and a private jet or yacht to ease the commute. What could be achieved if the amount were several times the price tags of all those luxuries? The end of world hunger or disease? Bill Gates, Microsoft's founder, decided he would aim to conquer malaria, ploughing a good slice of his near $100 billion personal fortune into that charitable endeavour. But the cash pile China is sitting on is even bigger than that. How about global domination? It would be tempting, even for those who aren't cast from the same mould as Blofeld. Money can buy power, lots of it, over allies and foes alike – even if, as China has found, it needs a bit of creative thinking.

Mingtian has lodged its dollar in China's Industrial and Commercial Bank, along with the required proof of how it was earned – i.e. through legitimate trade. Neatly besuited, with thinning hair and wire-rimmed glasses, its jovial chairman Yi Huiman looks every inch the bank manager. China's immense pile of export earnings means that the bank is the largest in the world, and Yi Huiman has the key to the vaults. He's been chairman only since 2016, but in his thirty-year career there he's seen the bank's fortunes explode.

And what will he to do with all the dollars that have been flowing in? Actually, this being China, he doesn't have much choice. He has to send them on to the central bank, to be exchanged for yuan at the rate it dictates. Mingtian gets its yuan; the PBC has its dollars. Those are then handed on to the State Administration of Foreign Exchange – which goes by the apt acronym of SAFE. What's it going to do with the money?

Whether it's Lauren Miller with a small savings stash for a rainy day, or SAFE sitting on piles of cash, one thing holds true for both. It's useless having money sitting idle. For one thing, as prices rise, it's going to go less far, buy fewer goods; its 'real' value will fall. It pays to put it to work.

Money may not buy happiness but it does buy choice. The more you have, the more options there are. Anyone with excess cash – that is, an investor – faces a lengthy and diverse menu of choices. What they choose, like any diner, depends on their budget, taste and appetite.

Fancy a fast-food option, something that might deliver a tasty morsel, or, equally, risks leaving you queasy? Equity – a share in a company – is the fried chicken of the investment world. The buyer owns a morsel of the company, and gets a side order of influence, or voting power, with it. Have a big appetite for influence? Order a large quantity of shares. Not that hungry for power? A small portion will do. If the share price rises, cash in your shares for a tasty bonus. Equally, the share price can fall and leave a nasty aftertaste.

A safer bet, albeit potentially less thrilling to the taste buds, is a classic dish: a government bond. Governments use bonds to finance their spending, topping up the money they get from taxes. It works like a loan. You buy the bit of paper, or bond, that the government issues, and it pays you interest. At the end of the loan's term, you get your money back. Bonds tend to offer low interest rates to investors as they're low risk but, generally, governments are good at paying back money. It's a relatively boring but safe choice.

Then there's the house special: a dish on which the restaurant is lavishing particular care. It might have to be ordered some time in advance and even paid for up front. This is a long-term investment, for example financing a building project. Investors have to wait to see how it turns out, salivating over the prospect of success. The outcome might, of course, not be as spectacular as hoped. There's always an element of risk.

Risk and the Chinese central bank aren't natural bedfellows. It's more usual for it to play the long game. The man dictating policy at the central bank, Zhou Xiaochuan, is not handing over that dollar lightly. The Chinese government staked its fortunes on becoming the world's assembly line, with the almighty dollar in its sights, and its attitude to its winnings is deeply conservative.

In the event, it decided the best thing to do was to send a lot of those dollars back to the USA. China has famously become a huge buyer of bonds issued by America, known as 'US treasuries'. For years, China had food envy as it watched the likes of Japan, which had been ordering this classic dish for a while. Now it is able to partake of the same meal.

In investment terms, low risk generally tends to mean low reward, but even 1 per cent of interest mounts up substantially when the investor is holding $3 trillion worth of these bonds, as China is. And they can easily be sold on if cash is needed.

The government of the world's biggest democracy is considered to be a pretty safe bet. Low risk, a decent return and easily cashed in. Small wonder that China has built up such a massive stake. But China's decision is more than just sound financial planning – there are strategic reasons to pick America and its dollar in particular.

The dollar's pole position was cemented in 1944 in a hotel in the New Hampshire mountains. A conference there aimed to establish international financial stability. The agreement – named after the hotel's location, Bretton Woods – was dominated by American officials. It named the dollar as the international reserve currency. That meant it was the official currency of global commerce, the one in which much international trade would be settled. And so the dollar became coveted by other countries. The value of most currencies was linked, or 'pegged', within a range of rates against the dollar. In turn the dollar's value was fixed against the value of gold. Strict controls were imposed on the transfer of funds to prevent this rigid system being upset. The International Monetary Fund was created, partly to police the number of dollars the USA printed. The idea was to ensure stability. But the system didn't work.

Those currency controls and the fixed exchange rates were largely relaxed in the early 1970s. As economies grew and diversified, the effort of keeping their currencies' prices stable proved to be impossibly complex and expensive. The system simply couldn't be sustained. It was not so different from what Thailand was to experience twenty-five years later.

One thing does remain, though: the dollar is still the chief reserve currency – it makes up 70 per cent of the cash held by central banks around the world – and the standard payment for trade. With the dollar remaining king, US government bonds are seen as the most prestigious and safest to own. There is speculation, however, that China's growing importance means that the yuan could push the dollar off the top of the currency tree. China's hoard gives it a safe, steady income to shore up its growing power base. It also gives it an element of control over America.

Let's look at it another way. American consumers such as Lauren Miller can't get enough of cheap Chinese goods. The Chinese government might then use her dollar to buy US treasuries. These bonds fund the American government, enabling it to build schools, pay pensions to the elderly and wages to the military. That keeps the cash swilling through the US economy, underpinning Lauren's weekly shop. So China 'owns' part of the US government's debt, and is funding its people. Americans keep spending, and China foots the bill.

Why does America dish up so many bonds to feed that machine? The truth is that it doesn't have much choice. Military action, a population that's growing older and needing pensions and healthcare, financial crises; none of it comes cheap. Over the years, America's government, like many others, has been in the unwelcome position of struggling to raise enough money through taxes to pay all its bills. Like most other countries, the USA would prefer to be able to balance its books. But it's had to take out loans, and its debts have grown. Bonds are a cheap way to borrow, much

cheaper than the average American's bank loan. And there's plenty of appetite for them from the likes of China.

That dollar might be printed in America and spent in a suburban Walmart, but it's debatable whether it belongs to Lauren Miller, Mingtian or the Chinese government.

Lauren Miller pays her mortgage in dollars, and she has China in part to thank for keeping the cost down. How? When there's a lot of demand for a government's bonds – as there is in China for US bonds – it pushes the price of the bond up, which means the government gets more cash up front for the same return. So the US government is paying less interest to borrow, and the Chinese 'lender' is getting a lower return, or yield. That is also reflected in the financial system as lower interest rates for ordinary Americans on borrowing such as mortgages. And those cheap Chinese imports are keeping down prices in the USA, which also helps to keep interest rates low.

Lauren Miller might see her actions as all-American, earning dollars locally and handing them over at her local supermarket to pay the wages of its staff, her neighbours. But her buying choices mean that the key factors determining her finances – from income to prices to interest rates – are influenced from many thousands of miles away.

Isn't that risky for the USA? What if China decided to throw in the towel and offload its bonds? Is it basically controlling the purse strings of the American economy? Could the US economy be held to ransom through geopolitical power play?

In 2016, China reshuffled its finances and offloaded $188 billion worth of bonds. It happened just as America elected President Trump, who had made no secret of his animosity towards China. The financial press was quick to run headlines such as 'America's biggest creditors dump treasuries in warning to Trump'. But those bonds easily found new homes. Debt with a price tag of eight or nine zeros changes hands but life in the aisles of Walmart and in offices across the USA carries on untroubled. China might have established itself as a linchpin of America's economy, but it's not alone; nor is it indispensable. As journalists at America's Bloomberg said, 'Relax. We'll survive China's sale of US debt.'

There are concerns over how big America's debt has grown. Encouraged by the appetite for its bonds, the US government has kept borrowing. Fortunately, however, its bonds remain in vogue across the planet, not just with China. Japan has long been a fan of the safe haven promised by US treasuries; China was just following its lead. Japan overtook China as the biggest collector of these pieces of paper in 2016, meaning it wields even greater power over the USA.

Hot on their heels, the next biggest holders of US bonds are far from superpowers. Around $230 billion worth were held in Ireland in 2016. It's even more eye-popping in the Cayman Islands. The tiny Caribbean territory, with 60,000 residents, is home to $265 billion of US treasuries. In both cases, though, it's not the central bank that owns these bonds, but companies. Extremely generous tax rules have made the Caymans and Ireland very popular as havens for hedge funds and other financial institutions, and even the ritziest of financial high-rollers need to park some money in safe places such as US treasuries. More on those high fliers of finance in Chapter 8.

But why is the investment going in only one direction, from China to the USA? China does have its own government bonds, as does Japan and most other countries. But China has been unusual in banning foreign ownership of its $9 trillion worth of bonds. The controller had no desire to be controlled – until July 2017, when Beijing announced it would be allowing such sales as part of a move to open up its money markets to attract foreign cash. This could be the start of a further shift in regional and global power.

The two countries might be locked into an uneasy mutual dependency but that doesn't mean China can hold the USA to ransom. There are plenty of other countries waiting in the wings to take its place, seeking influence and the security of America's bonds. But it just shows how linked we are all around the globe. Central bankers in Beijing or Tokyo can influence the fortunes of those wandering the aisles of Walmart, just as those American shoppers dictate fortunes in Shenzhen.

By accumulating all those dollars, China has given itself a huge amount of wealth and influence well beyond its shores. The more it earns, the more power it wields. However, it's an ever-changing game, with the likes of Vietnam and South Korea vying to chip away at China's export dominance.

China faces risks from all sides. If the USA is closely – some might say too closely – linked with China, which owns a lot of its debt, China is too closely linked to the markets for its goods. And that leaves it vulnerable. It's too reliant on the dollar. It's all about where the growth comes from, which is a challenge that every country faces. But what is growth? And how do you get it?

To grow an economy, you need to raise its income – or Gross Domestic Product (GDP). As the name suggests, GDP is the total of everything produced across a nation in a year: on farms, building sites, factories like Mingtian's and in offices, whether they're in private or government control. There are three ways of measuring GDP: adding up everything that's spent; everything that's produced; or everyone's earnings. There are plenty of options for ramping up GDP growth, or, in effect, making the country wealthier. Like identical triplets, no one of these measurements is superior, and each might show small variations. When you're calculating the output of millions of people and businesses, minor differences are inevitable.

China has focused on industry and manufacturing. It's all very well churning out the goods, but who's going to buy them? China's rising income may mean its workers have more consumer power, but its impact is still relatively modest compared to the dollar-waving American market. It makes sense to focus efforts on luring American consumers: not only are they able to buy more, but they can also – as with the iPhone – afford a higher price tag without much thought.

However, betting on wealthy overseas consumers to feather China's nest can be a risky strategy – a double-edged sword. Or, to confuse our metaphors further, as the saying goes in Beijing, 'Water can carry the boat and also overturn the boat.'

What happens if demand for exports dries up? In the aftermath of the 2008 financial crisis, global trade plunged between October 2008 and March 2009. For every six items sold previously, only five were being shifted by the end of that March. Demand from the USA, where the crisis had originated, was particularly badly hit. It was a lesson: while the Chinese government might always be able to rely on a market for US government bonds, it couldn't always rely on Lauren Miller splashing out on a payday treat in a supermarket. That's especially true if she is fearful about the family's next payday budget for the following month as well.

During the gold rush, Chinese factories and plants had sprung up like weeds; steel mills were working flat out. China was left producing more than it could sell. This being China, those affected were largely state-owned enterprises. The government was left with a costly headache, and stacks of unsold goods. It had to look closer to home to keep the fires of growth burning. The government decided it was time for the consumer to step up.

What the Chinese government wants is for its people to be more like Lauren Miller. They don't want them just to fork out on the basics, such as food and drink, but splash the occasional yuan on treats. It's that kind of spending that makes all the difference to growth in the economy as a whole. Chinese households have, on average, reached the point where that kind of frivolous spending is becoming affordable. And there's a huge reservoir to be tapped. Chinese households now earn about $5 trillion every year.

It's a huge shift in mindset for both the government and the Chinese people, and the result is that in China, over the first half of 2016, almost three quarters of growth came from the spending of its citizens. Vying for Lauren Miller's dollar by exporting a radio to the USA has taken a back seat. As incomes have risen, premium brands from abroad have become big business in China. Box-office receipts jumped 50 per cent in just one year. Travel abroad became a hot ticket: some 70 million Chinese took a trip overseas last year. China is now the world's largest carmaker. And it's the market for SUVs – the shiny gas-guzzlers synonymous with American con-sumerism – that's enjoyed the fastest success. What's more, for the first time, in 2015, the service sector – including shops, restaurants and the like – accounted for half the output in the economy.

This growing appetite in China can help the USA, too – though perhaps not those in Flint, Michigan. China has a trade surplus with the USA of $367 billion. This is also known as the country's *visible* balance of trade, because it covers those physical goods that are easily seen and counted. But there are other things that are traded across borders – primarily services – and China has a huge appetite for these *invisible* goods that America produces. There's Hollywood for starters: only thirty-four foreign films are approved to be shown on the big screen each year in China, but America's finest – and its flops – regularly sit at the top of the box-office charts. Takings at China's cinemas could overtake those in the USA within a few years, reflecting the sheer size of the audience. The USA is also earning from those Chinese tourists, who took advantage of their rising incomes to spend $250 billion on travel in 2015. Add in spending on education, software licenses, finance, and some other areas, and China is the fourth biggest foreign buyer of American services. In this trade area, the USA actually ran a surplus with China of $37 billion in 2016. That being said, overall, China is still running a surplus in what's known as its 'current account balance' with the USA, which is the total of all incomings and outgoings.

It's worth remembering, however, that most figures in economics are unlikely to be 100 per cent accurate. If you were to add up all the trade deficits and surpluses for all countries in the world they should balance out. But they don't. According to the IMF, the world had a current account surplus of almost $250 billion in 2015. How is that possible – unless we've been on an intergalactic shopping spree? The truth is that counting the value of cars and radios as they're shipped overseas is relatively easy, while accurately logging the value of every service that takes place is more difficult. There's always an element of error in trade figures: cash effectively lost down the back of the sofa.

Whether buying domestic products and services, or high-value imports, China's elite are starting to spend like Americans, because they are starting to earn like them. It's always hard to assess the exact fortunes of the wealthy, and that's especially so in a country as opaque as China. But the country was thought to have in excess of 1.5 million (dollar) millionaires in 2016. What of the super-rich? China has around 300 billionaires, with a new addition to the club every five days, according to bankers at UBS. In a sign of how it is transforming the global economy, two out of every three female self-made billionaires hail from China. The uber-rich make up a small but increasingly significant proportion of the population, and their reach is obvious. From Prada to Burberry via Chanel, one-third of luxury-brand sales are now made in China.

While the newly wealthy are wallowing in their designer watches and handbags, reshuffling China's growth may have come at a price. The amount of bad loans has risen sharply since 2010. It's the same kind of situation that led to the USA's and Europe's star power being dimmed by the 2008 global financial crisis. Media commentators across the globe worried that China might have learned from the West's successes but not taken heed of its failures.

Those risks aside, the impact of China's growing economic power becomes clearer as its consumers continue to flex their financial muscle and it grows as a market for other countries. However, China's massive reset on home turf isn't enough to satisfy its ambitions. With all those dollars earned from overseas comes the opportunity for power, and there are investments that bring in even higher financial rewards than shares or bonds. After all, there's a limit to how many bonds a country wants. Better still if this option can provide employment and business opportunities for your people, and perhaps a way to use machinery left idle after a fall in export demand.

It's time to ramp up investment overseas. This is an easy move for bank boss Yi Huiman, who has seen plenty of foreign firms profiting from building offices and factories in China. Increasingly, China is deciding that it too wants to be one of these players, and take a slice of the action elsewhere.

Global trade links aren't new. The original Silk Road was a network of trade routes established over two thousand years ago under the Han Dynasty in China. It linked the trading regions of the ancient world, east to west. In the twenty-first century, President Xi Jinping has unveiled his own New Silk Road to cement China's might. It's intended, he claims, to forge a path of peace, inclusiveness and free trade, to do away with the trade wars of old and introduce a new form of economic diplomacy. The plan centres on building a network of roads, railways, ports, power plants and fuel pipelines connecting China with South-East and Central Asia, the Middle East, Africa and Europe – backed by Chinese money. Is China building bridges or, as the country's critics would have it, using its new riches to spread its control?

As with all foreign travel to far-flung places, it's a venture packed with excitement – and risk. That risk has been quite a change for China, but one it has embraced. This means our dollar isn't destined to stay tucked in the vaults in Beijing Financial Street. It's packed and ready for the next stage of its journey: hopping back through seven time zones to Nigeria, where it'll be taking to the railway on a voyage of discovery.

3

Finding love in the Niger Delta

China to Nigeria

The ancient port city of Calabar lies tucked into the south-eastern corner of Nigeria. Idyllic and serene, it boasts botanic gardens, museums and wildlife sanctuaries, but behind the pretty façade Calabar has a dark history. Between the seventeenth and nineteenth centuries it was a major slave port, a key hub in human trafficking. That sordid chapter is documented in the Calabar Slave Museum. Today, though, Calabar focuses on being a centre for tourism and fun. Its annual carnival is hailed as the 'biggest street party in Africa'.

Some 6,936 miles from Beijing, Calabar is where China is send-ing some of its dollars. It might seem an oddly frivolous choice. But the PBC isn't here to party or soak up the sun: each dollar is part of a meticulously planned investment decision that promises power as well as cash in return. This kind of attention isn't new for the town. Even the eighteenth-century Western presence in West Africa, the forerunner of colonialism, can be seen as an investment decision, designed to capitalise on Nigeria's commodities. Only then the commodity was humans: slaves. Now, once again, Calabar finds itself a player in world trade.

The city lies five hundred miles from Nigeria's financial capital, Lagos, and it is one of the beneficiaries of the vast quantities of dollars that are flowing from China into Africa. In 2014, the Nigerian government signed a $12 billion contract with the China Railway Construction Corporation to build a coastal railway linking the two cities, and the money largely came in the form of loans from China. Those funds were from the vaults of banks such as the Industrial and Commercial Bank of China – where the Shenzhen radio-maker banked the dollar it received from Lauren Miller.

The railway isn't intended simply to provide the elite of Lagos with a convenient coastal route. The twenty-two-station line will cross ten of Nigeria's thirty-six states. That includes, most significantly, the oil-producing Niger Delta region. Nigeria pumped up to 2 million barrels of oil per day in 2016. It's a vast amount, but it wasn't enough for Nigeria to rank as one of the top-ten oil producers that year, alongside the likes of Saudi Arabia or even Canada. However, it's not the quantity of Nigeria's oil that counts. It's the quality. This is some of the highest-grade oil on the planet, much coveted for use in cars and planes. Calabar's railway will connect Nigeria's economic capital to the heart of its production zone. It came about through the government's grand twenty-five-year plan, Nigeria Vision 2020, which aimed to make the West African country one of the foremost economies in the world. And China is lending a helping hand.

❧

Why is China choosing to put its dollar into a railway on the other side of the globe? It's a lot of cash to entrust to a project far from home and with little obvious benefit to China's own people.

China is on a quest to go global. The scale of its investments overseas has exploded over the last decade. In 2014, for the first time, its overseas investments exceeded the investments reaching its shores. Our dollar is among billions of others in Nigeria, mostly from state-owned enterprises choosing to spend China's money abroad.

China is now ranked in the top three sources of overseas investment. And its interests are certainly diverse. Let us set aside Nigerian railways for the moment. British football clubs such as Aston Villa, Wolverhampton Wanderers and West Bromwich Albion are now held by Chinese oligarchs. Chinese conglomerates own the makers of films such as *Godzilla*. Flight comparison website Skyscanner is now in the hands of a Chinese company. One of New York's most iconic hotels, the Waldorf Astoria, was sold to the Chinese, destined to be partly converted into luxury condos. Lifting a football cup is one way of demonstrating that China has truly arrived as a leading protagonist on the world stage, but these are trophy assets, almost vanity projects.

More important to its long-term ambitions are China's strategic investments. It has key stakes in European power stations and water providers. It's even got money in retirement homes in America. China is wielding its power globally to exercise control and make money from the fundamentals of life. The continuation of society is reliant on basics including energy and water, and populations, particularly in the affluent West, are ageing fast.

These are just a few examples of China's foreign forays. China is spreading its dollars in fields ranging from property to entertainment, from consumer goods to infrastructure, displaying its vast and varied ambitions beyond the conveyor belt of low-value manufacturing that built its fortune.

This has left many observers uneasy. These kinds of projects are termed 'foreign direct investment' (FDI). It's most likely to involve the purchase of buildings or something tangible, but it could also mean buying a significant stake in a company in another country. The common characteristic of all types of FDI is that it gives the investor some control, whether the investment is in a factory, a railway or a company.

The amount China spent on acquisitions in Europe in 2016 was four times as much as investment in the other direction. As China's spending spree continues, there's growing opposition to this activity, not least because China is placing barriers in the way of foreign interests controlling its own key industries. This is leaving a trail of ownership that has been dubbed the New Silk Road. Europe took a knock from the 2008 financial crisis and the money China invested has plugged many a gap.

On a relatively frivolous level, eyebrows were raised when one of Britain's iconic brands, Weetabix, fell into Chinese hands in 2012. Would it still taste the same? What would a nation that was more accustomed to barbecue pork buns for breakfast want with a wholewheat cereal of flaky biscuits? In the event, Chinese shoppers wouldn't bite and so Weetabix was sold on to an American company in 2017. At a more serious level, China has also been backing new power stations in the UK, and buying stakes in its water companies. There are worries that letting China have control over such sensitive and vital areas leaves a country vulnerable, both financially and strategically. There are concerns that foreign owners will run companies – even in less critical industries – to earn profits for backers at home, cost-cutting at the expense of local workers and customers. There may be many thousands of miles separating Nigeria and Britain but, as we shall see, many of the concerns over China's investment are the same.

The global map of ownership and control has changed drastically over the last seventy-five years and there are now flows of FDI everywhere. Until the mid-twentieth century, countries with funds to spend and invest overseas – most prominently former empire-builders such as the USA, the UK and France – were located largely in the West. They were able to profit, both financially and in terms of economic power, from trade with their commodity-rich territories. The dissolution of those empires was followed by an increased need for oil for transport and industry and the rising price of this vital commodity. This created the oil barons of the Middle East, with their vastly influential funds. Oil-rich states such as Saudi Arabia and Norway tend to be awash in surplus cash – 'sovereign wealth funds' – which typically cast a roving eye around the globe looking for a place to reap rewards and influence.

Then there's the money that all of us rapidly ageing workers are putting aside for our retirement: the pension funds. The fund needs to grow, but we are probably not planning to draw on that money for many years, so its managers may be happy to fund longer-term, perhaps ultimately more rewarding (and safer) projects, rather than just look to make a quick buck. The biggest employers in the richest areas tend to have the most funds. Topping the list are Japan's and the USA's public employee funds. The deepening pockets and ambitions of pension funds has led to Canadian teachers – or rather their pension savings – supplying Nigeria's offshore oilfields with mooring cables via a company they own. Nigeria's fortunes are literally tethered to theirs. However, the members of that pension fund are not interested in control; more important to them is a decent return.

So where is all of that FDI money destined to end up? The most popular destinations for global investors in 2016 included the world's biggest shoppers – and those feeding their appetite to spend. The USA took pole position while China was third, with the UK sandwiched in between. (Why the tiny UK? That was down to a rash of big company takeovers, including the creation of the world's largest beer producer.) Underlining how much investors like to place their dollars on a safe bet, established commodity-rich markets such as the Netherlands, Brazil and Australia also feature in the top ten. For all its oil, Nigeria doesn't feature in the top tiers.

The transfer of every dollar demands in return some surrender of profit and power. Growing international movements of funds bring shifts in ownership and economic control. China's foray into Nigeria is more than part of a quest to corner the global railway-construction market. It's a key part of China's New Silk Road plan, building infrastructure to boost trade links on both sides. China hopes to reap the benefits – financial and otherwise – far beyond the tracks.

The chairman of China Railway Construction Corporation described the Nigerian railway as a 'mutually beneficial project'. He stated it would allow China to export $4 billion worth of equipment – from steel to trains – to Nigeria. The construction of the railway provides ready contracts and work for Chinese firms. It's a further step in China's plan to move its manufacturing industry towards the higher-tech, higher-skilled and higher-value end of the scale. It's all part of a bid to take over similar projects across the globe.

But when it comes to China's interest in Nigeria, all roads – or railways, in this case – lead to oil and to raw materials. China is not alone in this; almost half the money invested in Africa from elsewhere is chasing commodities, including diamonds and cobalt, which is a key component for smartphones.

For the Chinese bank, investing in Nigeria is about power and influence. Yet China has hardly needed to fight off the competition from multinational companies, banks or other wealthy governments to land the Nigerian infrastructure projects it's sunk its dollars into.

Much of the FDI going into Nigeria comes from oil firms, including Anglo-Dutch giant Shell and America's ExxonMobil. Despite Nigeria's wealth of natural resources and potential, many other investors don't want to back the country's projects. For them, the risk involved is too much; they've decided there's a good chance they wouldn't even get their initial investment back, let alone reap any extra benefits.

If you're a wealthy nation or a private company, choosing where to invest your money is not unlike internet dating. There are plenty of options out there. When it comes to dating, you're basically rating candidates on a number of factors: looks, sense of humour, shared beliefs and whether they remember to put the top back on the toothpaste. Then you rank how important each of those attributes is to you. It might be a clinical process, but work through the scorecard and the perfect match might be the payback.

For potential investors, the process is the same. All they want, too, is a rewarding and harmonious (and hopefully lasting) relationship with an attractive and compatible partner for their dollar. But they have to weigh up a different set of factors before they weed out the toads and find Prince or Princess Charming. It's risk versus reward.

Are they looking for a long-distance relationship, to build a base far from home as China is doing, or a less risky one nearer home? How attractive is the project? Is it high profile? Does it promise a big financial return and also provide business and jobs for the folks back home, as the coastal railway does? Is it risky? What's the political climate like? Can you trust the government with your cash or will it change the rules or regulations in a way that hurts your investment? How bright are the prospects, weighed up against the uncertainty? Is the country prone to unrest? These are just a few of the things investors have to consider.

A rich seam of resources and a captive market for its manufactured goods were what drew the UK to Nigeria in the nineteenth century, just as they prompted other European nations to colonise countries across Africa. It's the same kind of attraction that Nigeria holds for China now, except in the nineteenth century it was a different type of oil – palm oil – that was the main draw. Palm oil could be fashioned into soap, and keep machines turning back in Europe for the colonial masters. But in the quest to pump as many raw materials – such as cocoa, oil and coffee – as possible out of Africa, the West failed to develop other areas, or share its industrial knowledge. Roads and railways were built but only where they served the needs of the economic masters. The wealth and power were concentrated in a few sectors and in a few hands. When the various empires collapsed in the mid-twentieth century, the resulting scrabble for power resulted in wide-reaching ethnic and regional conflict.

Consequently, Nigeria has become as well known for political instability, abuses of power, corruption and civil unrest as it has for its oilfields. Ironically, that's what's made much of the West scratch Nigeria off its list of potential partners, and kept China on its toes. Its size and oil reserves make Nigeria the most extreme example, but the same colonial legacy holds for many other countries in the region, where risk is, to a lesser degree, sometimes seen to outweigh reward. Substitute cocoa, coffee or tea for palm oil, and Ghana and Kenya could tell similar stories. The lure of natural resources is tempered by the reality and perception of political stability and security concerns.

The second half of the twentieth century in Nigeria was peppered with military dictatorships. Democratic rule returned in 1999 but that didn't mean the end of instability and unrest. Nor did it quell claims of corruption and the misappropriation of funds, even at the highest official levels. As in colonial times, the power and wealth derived from the oilfields are the province of only a few elite Nigerians and the foreign companies. They include Shell, ExxonMobil, Eni, Chevron and Total: the fuel titans of the West. President Buhari, elected in 2015, promised to clamp down on corruption and push through economic reforms, yet many remain sceptical.

The World Bank claims that four out of every five dollars earned by the energy sector benefit just 1 per cent of the Nigerian population. Resentment, poverty and disaffection have stirred up not only militants in the south of the country but also raised tension between ethnic groups. The unrest erupted into violence and attacks on oil pipelines and facilities. The threat of kidnapping has led foreign oil companies to spend a fortune on security: staff are housed in fortress camps, apartment blocks, even compounds funded by their employers. These gated communities can contain everything from hotels to schools and restaurants. They sometimes encompass an entire suburb, hermetically sealed against local life and awash with state-of-the-art fittings, SUVs, air conditioning and so on. It's a far cry not just from the typical Nigerian experience but also from lifestyles back home. These are echoes of colonialism, but the emphasis is on security more than on luxury. The workers have to be paid more – danger money – to accept the risks Nigeria poses to their safety. Even a trip to the airport demands an armed convoy. These employees are constant targets.

Nigeria is still a very unequal, disparate country. Roughly half the population is Muslim, dwelling largely in the north. The non-Muslims, for the most part Christian, are more likely to be found in the oil-rich region of the south. However, that doesn't necessarily mean that the Nigerians living there enjoy the spoils. The ethnic and religious tensions have spilled over into political ones as power has shifted between the camps.

In the north, the government faces increasing threat from Boko Haram extremists, who made international headlines when they abducted more than two hundred schoolgirls from Chibok in 2014. The jihadist group's quest for a caliphate has provoked a humanitarian crisis, displacing close to 2 million people. Meanwhile, in the south, oil production has been severely disrupted by insurgent attacks on pipelines. Even with the Chinese supplying military equipment and training for its armed forces, the Nigerian government is facing enormous challenges.

Add a hefty tax system and volatile oil prices, and even the most well-heeled energy companies can find business in Nigeria both stressful and costly. The long-distance relationship can quickly become high-maintenance. China is, however, prepared to put up with the country's issues if it means gaining influence over a reliable source of black gold. As its factories have fired up, and the nation has taken to the roads, China's become the world's largest user of oil. It has to ensure it can get the oil it needs to keep its vast engines of production running. It's impossible to be a manufacturing kingpin without ready access to oil. China's big competitors – the USA, even parts of Europe – usually have their own oil, or at least supplies on tap from long-standing allies. China, largely, has to find its own, so turns a blind eye to Nigeria's problems. It's a bit like dating a bad boy because he has a flash car.

There's a reason China has such easy access to Nigeria's oil stores. Nigeria's oil infrastructure was creaking. Its four refineries aren't up to scratch. Nigeria can pump the sticky crude oil out of the ground but it can't process it. Ironically it has to import over 80 per cent of the refined oil its people and businesses need, at much higher cost. Enter China, with a promise of $80 billion to repair and build refineries, pipelines and other facilities. After some gentle wooing, it is not surprising that China's companies have raced to the front of the queue to be granted drilling rights to some of Nigeria's most lucrative oil reserves. Not only does that mean China can more easily get its hands on the kind of oil it needs but that it can also profit from its sale to others. This kind of investment in turn entices Nigeria to continue developing its oil sector. It strives to pump more of the black stuff, which China is waiting to lap up. In 2015, China bought one million barrels from Nigeria, a small fraction of its output. But China says it wants more – much more.

In future, Nigeria can expect to be love-bombed with more funds from the same source. As he unveiled the latest tranche of investment, China's foreign minister Wang Yi said, 'Compared with the size, population and market of our two countries, our cooperation still has large potential to be deepened.' China's reserves are likely to be tapped up for more dollars.

However, Nigeria could yet find its admirer getting itchy feet. As growth has slowed, demand for oil has softened in China. That's prompted it to look around and rumour has it that China may be shining its spotlight on Latin America next. The announcement that China was to build Nigeria's high-speed railway came just after Mexico rejected a similar deal. FDI is a fickle business; the next dollar could find itself chasing the next hot model in a different continent altogether.

Nigeria may not be up there with the leading global players but it's the second-biggest magnet for foreign money in sub-Saharan Africa, after Angola. It attracts much of the big bucks and headlines due to its oil, and it assiduously courts this investment, as do many of its neighbours. Ethiopia is also creeping up the ranks of nations attracting overseas investment. It may not have oil but it has other commodities, and it's a populous nation which makes it an attractive bet, with an increasing amount of money coming in from sectors such as financial services, telecoms and technology. There is a common theme, though: the projects promise money for some, but they don't ensure mass job creation. All developing countries have to overcome some of the same obstacles as Nigeria: reassuring foreigners not just about the prospects for growth, but also about the ease of doing business and political stability. Ethiopia, in particular, is trying to attract funds for an ambitious dam on the Nile. That kind of major infrastructure project is not just bread and butter for foreign investors; it's the road to prosperity for poorer nations.

The Minister of Transportation hailed the Calabar railway as a 'key corridor' of Nigeria's strategy. That's no exaggeration. It's no good having the potential to produce what the world wants to buy if it's costly and complex to make or extract, and customers can't get their hands on it at the right price. That means having the right infrastructure, including schools, energy, communications systems and transport links.

Transport in Nigeria has long been crying out for improvement. At the start of the millennium, the country had just two major railway lines, both able only to chug away at low speed and in varying states of disrepair. Nigeria's roads bore the brunt of the freight industry and that took its toll. Their state of disrepair and congestion has slowed traffic considerably. Trains on the new railway would run at 80 miles per hour, halving the current twelve-hour road trip between Calabar and Lagos. Besides connecting the two commercial centres, the railway will, Nigeria's government claimed, transport 50 million passengers per year. Its construction would create 200,000 jobs, according to its Chinese partners. That's very welcome in a country where job creation has not kept up with explosive population growth, particularly in the cities. For Nigeria, each dollar received matters. It might sound a trivial amount but when six out of ten people in the population have less than that to live on per day, it all counts.

The country has a long way to go to achieve its economic potential. Oil has dominated the story – and Nigeria's earnings – for too long. The country might once have been a leading exporter of cocoa and palm oil, but the focus on oil means those industries have been allowed to decay. Two out of every three Nigerians still work in agriculture. Nigeria could be a major exporter of food but with little attention to this sector there's been no progress in productivity – the amount each worker can produce in an hour or a day. Despite its own natural resources, Nigeria has to ship in food to feed its booming population. Improved rail links could vastly help. But even if it had the cash – which it doesn't – Nigeria doesn't have the expertise to build high-speed railways.

The payback to Nigeria from that dollar of investment is clear. It might also help to spread the wealth of the oil sector a little further. At present, 60 per cent of Nigeria's 180 million people live in poverty on less than a dollar per day. China's actions might help to put a bit more money in their pockets, and that benefits both parties: China aims to use its growing influence in Nigeria to help channel that money into the pockets of its own manufacturers.

Traditional, colourful Ankara print fabric peppers the length of Lagos's main market. A yard of it costs about a dollar. For a material that's frequently used in bulk for wedding or funeral attire the modest cost is an advantage. But the design is all that's likely to be traditional about it. The fabric itself might well have been made in China, a lower-quality but more affordable alternative to homespun options. It's put local producers out of business. The same is true for other products: for example, the machinery used in factories, where China is increasingly replacing European suppliers. As in America, China is exerting its muscle to undercut local producers and international competitors, to the advantage of shoppers.

The Chinese banker's dollar promises access to and influence over Nigeria's oil and consumer market, and work for its manufacturers. But can it buy Nigerian hearts too? To meet its needs, China realises sugar works better than vinegar; hospitality and gentle wooing trump hostility. The railway, it hopes, will give its nation – and products – good PR with ordinary Nigerians. China has been looking to ramp up its 'soft power' with Nigeria. This kind of power is the ultimate weapon in a twenty-first-century state's foreign policy if it wants to draw ahead on the global stage.

China has been building its diplomatic and political ties with the West African nation since 1971. While the West backed away during Nigeria's military dictatorships, China strengthened its ties with its ally. China has its own chequered human rights record, which gives it a comparative advantage as it is not troubled by the behaviour of other countries. As only good friends can, China provided the Nigerian government with military assistance during insurgencies in the Niger Delta. Nigeria in return gave its explicit, written support to China's attempts to stake a claim over Taiwan.

On a smaller, but still vital, scale, the two countries have formed cultural and educational links, from reciprocal film festivals to student exchanges, with varying success. More productive has been the relationship between Nigeria's Television Authority and Chinese tech specialist StarTimes, which has resulted in a digital pay TV service. For a little over a dollar per month, Nigerians can access dozens of channels, thanks to China.

In 2014, a BBC survey found that Nigeria was the country most favourably disposed towards China; others were put off by China's human rights records and perceptions of its power-hungry, even bullying, actions. Nigeria is the biggest overseas customer of Chinese construction companies. It's handy timing for those companies, as demand slows at home. The relationship between China and Nigeria seems firmly established; a union built on mutual financial benefit and growing influence. If this were a traditional fairy tale, it might be the point where they start to live happily ever after.

But all fairy tales have their darker sides, and the union has not only been far from smooth in the past but is likely to remain so. Is there a downside for Nigeria? A much-needed injection of cash into its crumbling or non-existent infrastructure boosts living standards, at least for some. Does it matter that it is China and not the Nigerian government that is producing the cash? It does. In return Nigeria is giving up some power and influence over its own future.

The focus on oil puts Nigeria under immense pressure to extract and refine, at whatever cost. This is happening at the expense of the development of its already neglected agricultural or manufacturing sectors. In an ideal world, this kind of investment would equip Nigeria with technology to enable a more knowledgeable, productive workforce. It might, if the wealth were shared equally rather than just residing with those at the top. But when China builds railways, its investment can be seen as facilitating its own high-tech businesses and workers, rather than as an opportunity to upskill local workers.

As tensions in the north of Nigeria intensify, millions face the prospect of famine. The country can't feed itself, and Chinese money isn't enabling a sustainable path towards prosperity. The colonial legacy continues. Meanwhile, there are hundreds of oil spills in the Niger Delta every year, bringing ecological disaster.

The governments of both countries would say theirs is a thriving relationship of beneficial interdependence. A flourishing superpower is helping another country to reach its potential by bridging an ideas gap. Elsewhere, there have been cries of exploitation and Chinese imperialism. Lamido Sanusi, former governor of Nigeria's central bank, says it's reminiscent of the colonialism of old, with China taking Nigeria's raw materials and selling it manufactured goods, without enriching the country with skills or jobs. China's Wang Yi disagrees, saying, 'We absolutely will not take the old path of Western colonists.'

༄

Although it slipped to $3.1 billion in 2015, as falling oil prices bit, FDI has overtaken the amount Nigeria gets in overseas aid. However, not much of our dollar will trickle down to improve the living standards of the bulk of the population. The effect the dollar has in Nigeria is potentially a thorny issue.

But should Nigeria rely on Chinese investment to improve the welfare of Nigerians? Isn't that the job of Nigeria's government? Perhaps, but from failures of governance and economic mismanagement to a lack of funds caused by the falling oil price, it's clear the government has long failed to deliver. Should aid have a role to play in filling that gap?

Welfare is about much more than just the average level of income in a country. This is particularly true in Nigeria, where a few people measure their income in hundreds of millions while the majority earns only a few hundred dollars a year. Add up all those incomes, divide it by the number of people, and it gives a misleading idea of how well off the 'average' Nigerian is. To assess development, or well-being, the World Bank looks at a number of other features too, from life expectancy to access to clean water and literacy. Nigerians born today can typically expect to live to the age of fifty-three. Fewer than four out of five complete primary school. Over a quarter of the population – more than 40 million people – can't access clean water. A country with a rich seam of natural resources and a massive, young population could do far better.

The World Bank was set up not just to log statistics but also to promote a better future for countries such as Nigeria. Its upfront aim is to 'end extreme poverty within a generation and boost shared prosperity'. It's ambitious stuff. In cold, hard, cash terms, that means loans and grants to support long-term projects as well as providing emergency support. Other international non-governmental organisations – NGOs – carrying out similar work include the United Nations, the International Monetary Fund (IMF) and the African Development Bank.

Then there are funds that come in via the international charities – from the biggest multinational players, such as Oxfam and the Red Cross, to the smaller bodies supporting local initiatives – and the amounts pledged by the governments of richer countries including the UK and USA. Together, all these sources supplied Nigeria with close to $2.5 billion in 2015.

When asked to think of aid directed to sub-Saharan Africa, those old enough to remember the 1980s will immediately think of the harrowing photos of famine-ravaged Ethiopia that prompted a global string of songs and concerts under the Live Aid banner. That a further benefit-raising concert was held to mark Live Aid's twentieth anniversary under the slogan 'Make Poverty History' underlines the fact that many of the humanitarian problems remained unresolved in 2005. In Nigeria, the need for humanitarian aid has continued into the twenty-first century. At the start of 2017, the UN needed to get food to almost 3 million people in the north-east of the country, where neglect, drought, chronic poverty and Boko Haram had created the threat of famine. The situation highlighted the need to provide farming communities with seeds, tools and help to replace destroyed resources in time for the planting season, to prevent a lasting cycle of crop failure and hunger.

Most of the aid reaching Nigeria's shores is earmarked for longer-term infrastructure projects, bolstering the less fashionable or lucrative areas not reached by foreign investment. By filling in the gaps, the idea is to enable Nigeria to gather the tools it needs to fulfil its potential in the global economy.

How much of a difference has aid made to Nigeria? Despite its oil wealth, the country continues to languish when it comes to improving the well-being and prosperity of its population. There have been some triumphs, though, including stemming the spread of HIV. The World Bank part funded a much needed public transport system for Lagos, which, with its population of over 20 million and rising, is the biggest city in sub-Saharan Africa. While the project proved hugely beneficial even to poorer sections of the population, the World Bank deemed it only 'moderately satisfactory', not least because the cost had more than doubled by the time the project was completed.

Critics are quick to point out that aid funds can easily be misappropriated on the ground. And those projects are sometimes ill conceived to start with. Over $100 million was donated by the UK to help privatise Nigeria's energy system; the results included higher prices, job losses and blackouts. Aid or loans might also come with conditions attached: orders to reform the economy in ways that might not seem to be in the interest of the people. Such conditionality is often the way of bodies such as the IMF, and it has been criticised as a well-meaning but misguided 'one size fits all' approach that can be harmful in itself.

Others have accused aid donors of 'spoon-feeding' countries, creating a culture of dependency. They say the offer of easy money means a government doesn't have the incentive to keep its house in order, channel its export income efficiently and ensure the economy is set up to provide for its own.

For every success story, there's another showing that aid isn't compensating for the shortfalls left by investment. It just underlines how there's no blueprint for poorer countries to beat poverty and raise livings standards to equal those enjoyed by their richer neighbours. In fact, the countries that are most 'blessed' with resources such as oil might struggle the most with those gifts – as we shall see later with Iraq and Russia.

Why is China, or anyone else, investing in Nigeria in dollars? Why, in a deal between China and Nigeria, are we referring to a currency belonging to a country on the other side of the planet? Why not renminbi, the Chinese currency, or the naira, Nigeria's own currency? Quite simply, the dollar is the common global financial lingo, the standard currency of invoicing for trade and investment. Its value is easy to understand; it's reliable, easy to use . . . it's the steadfast boy-next-door intermediary in this courtship between two less established but in many ways more exciting partners.

Nigeria pays for the vast majority of its imports – from food to textiles – in dollars. It's not alone in this: almost every country sees the value of the trade it conducts in dollars exceed the amount of its trade with America. That's partly because commodities are priced in dollars. But one dollar in every five Nigeria spends on imports of goods goes to China, making it the West African nation's biggest trading partner, even before taking into account Chinese investment in rail and pipelines. Oil may be paid for in dollars but not everything has to be. Doesn't it make more sense to cut out the dollar, and deal in national currencies?

Moves towards doing just that were made in 2015. The central banks of both countries agreed to make funds available in each of their currencies to pay for imports from the other country. It's known as a currency swap, and it's the kind of deal China has been making more frequently in recent years, as it tries to assert the might of its own currency. Or, as China would claim, to facilitate trade and stabilise markets.

Goodbye, dollars? Not quite yet. It's a significant but small start, but most goods arriving in Nigeria from international sellers are still paid for in dollars. Meanwhile, with all that investment and aid, there remain a few billion dollars flowing into Nigeria every year. Nigeria's central bank likes to keep a tight grip on dollars, as does China's, because in Nigeria, whether the government likes it or not, the dollar is king.

For years, as expensive oil flowed out of Nigeria, a plentiful supply of dollars flowed in. If people wanted Nigerian oil, they needed Nigeria's currency to buy it. This kept the naira's price – the exchange rate against the dollar – high. But then the oil price dropped, and by early 2016 it had slumped to an eleven-year low. Cheaper oil means fewer dollars and less demand for the naira, which should mean a fall in the exchange rate. The naira would be worth less and if Nigerians wanted to buy dollars it would cost them a lot more.

The obvious – and easiest – thing for the government to do would be to let the currency drift down. That was what other oil-producing countries were doing. The government was forced to let the value of the currency drop somewhat: the naira had lost over 25 per cent of its value in the six months to February 2015, by which time $1 would get you 198 nairas, compared to about 160 previously. Controversially however, Nigeria's government resisted going further. Its reasoning was that a weaker naira meant a weaker country. It argued a lower exchange rate pushes up the price of imports (which is true), increasing the cost of living – especially in Nigeria, which is so reliant on goods from abroad.

Instead, the government decided that now was the time to persuade Nigerians to buy Nigerian, and to step up production where it had been lacking before. It's a philosophy repeated around the world – a growing backlash against the impact of globalisation as countries stand up for the interests of their own. But Nigeria took a fairly unusual approach. The central bank drew up a list of forty-one items – from rice to private jets – that it would no longer supply dollars to import.

In China, the central bank kept a close grip on dollars because it wanted to control its exchange rate, to stop it rising too fast. Its Nigerian counterpart, however, did so simply to protect its fast-dwindling pile of dollar reserves when it saw fewer dollars coming into the country. The dollar is the currency Nigeria needs to conduct the core part of its global business. The shortage was effectively holding Nigeria to ransom.

But, as China could have warned Nigeria, holding back dollars can be counterproductive: it pushes down your own currency. The government's move just exacerbated the naira problem.

In Nigeria, those whose livelihoods depend on buying from abroad face invoices priced in dollars. They were determined to get hold of dollars to make their purchases. Cue the black market. They turned to the back-alley shops and their electronic online equivalents. With dollars in short supply, it cost more and more nairas to get hold of one – around 400 in 2016, a far cry from the artificial 'official exchange rate' of closer to 300.

Meanwhile, the import restrictions meant a shortage of raw materials for factories, and gaps on supermarket shelves. Prices soared, with the blame levelled at 'the dollar problem'. Some airlines, such as America's United and Spain's Iberia, stopped flights to Nigeria, as they were unable to convert the money they were earning from ticket sales in the country into dollars.

The Nigerian government was clutching its dollars very close to its chest. And that wasn't just a drain on Nigerians' resources; it was a drain on the government's economic credibility, and promoted smuggling and corruption. Already deterred by the weaker oil price, foreign investors backed away further. Trying to keep a grip on the almighty dollar was costing the country dear and, in turn, keeping the dollars away.

The agreement with the Chinese to enable nairas to be swapped for renminbi helped to take the edge off the crisis – slightly. But the chaos mounted and, in June 2016, the government supposedly stopped the restrictions. The exchange rate promptly dropped sharply towards the black-market rate, better reflecting the demand for the scarce supply of dollars. Ironically, the determination to promote the naira has made it more likely that the dollar will be the trusted currency of Nigeria for longer. Its power remains.

Nor did the currency crisis itself persuade Nigerians to buy Nigerian. Jollof rice can be described as Nigeria's national dish (although some claim it originated in Senegal); no party is complete without it. It consists of a sauce based on tomatoes, peppers and onions, and, of course, rice. Such is the popularity of rice, sacks of it are exchanged as Christmas presents. In any market, much of the rice on sale is likely not to be Nigerian. About half of the 5 million tonnes eaten in Nigeria comes from abroad. That's despite a doubling in the price of an imported bag, owing to duty of 60 per cent and the impact of the naira crisis.

Nigeria's rice industry has struggled to meet the country's needs. It's beset with obstacles, such as a lack of infrastructure, from roads to warehouses and distribution systems. Farms tend to be relatively small, and farmers have lacked access to the cheap loans needed to expand, buy machinery and bump up crop yield, which, in turn, has held back production. President Buhari made rice production a priority, and claimed that by the end of 2017 the country would be self-sufficient. It was a very ambitious target.

For the time being, then, that bag of rice is likely to have come from India or Thailand. Customers in Nigeria will be paying in naira, but the retailer from whom they are buying their rice will have bought it wholesale from a foreign supplier and paid in dollars.

In any case, not even the currency crisis could convince Nigerians to buy Nigerian rice. Foreign rice was largely perceived as being of better quality, even healthier, than the homegrown crop. Better-off Nigerians are prepared to pay for it, even if the cost has soared. While Lauren Miller in Walmart focused on the price, a Nigerian customer views this purchase as a status symbol.

Imported rice remains part of daily life in Lagos. Importers are able to convince the central bank to part with a few of its dollars to spend on the ingredients for Nigeria's national dish. That dollar is sent from Nigeria's central bank to a middleman representing rice farmers many thousands of miles away. The desire for proper Jollof rice means our dollar is heading east again, this time for India.

4

Spicing up the recipe for success

Nigeria to India

In India, our dollar is being spent on a grass, one that's sustained more humans for longer than any other crop: *Oryza sativa*. It's better known as rice. The cultivation of rice is believed to have originated in ancient China, and has since ventured further afield. Today, one in five bowls of rice eaten around the world comes from India.

With 7.6 billion mouths on this planet, that's a lot of rice. Agriculture isn't a fashionable industry but it's crucial to human survival. The land potentially available for cultivating crops or grazing livestock is, of course, in fixed supply, but our population certainly isn't; over this century it's predicted to triple. Even as farming becomes more efficient, that's quite a challenge.

As it is, around one in eight of the world's population is undernourished. Is this because we are unable to produce enough food, or is it rather that we cannot get it to the right places, matching supply and demand? We all need to eat; whether we are all able to afford to is another matter. Those with the biggest waistlines are also the richest on the planet – Americans and Europeans – and the smallest eaters are those in the most impoverished corners of sub-Saharan Africa. Lauren Miller in Texas spends about 20 per cent of her income on feeding herself; Nigerians spend 56 per cent.

What is eaten differs, too. The poorer you are the more likely you are to rely on starchy staples such as rice, while increased affluence has allowed the Chinese, for example, to enjoy meat, dairy and vegetables more often. The arrival of McDonald's can be a sign that a developing country has 'made it', although in jaded America the golden arches are viewed warily as a harbinger of obesity. Globally, a growing population – disproportionately in the poorer countries of Asia and Africa – with rising incomes means that prices too are rising. The Organisation for Economic Co-operation and Development (OECD) estimates that our food supply needs to rise by 70 per cent by 2050. There could be greater shortages ahead. Food – and the ability to grow it or afford it – may equal power.

Typically, rice is grown by flooding fields at the same time or shortly after the planting of young seedlings. The final crop comes in many forms: short, sticky, long grain. Perhaps the best known to come from India is basmati – 'fragrant' in Hindi. But, as any discerning West African chef knows, for authentic Jollof you need non-basmati long-grain parboiled rice. And it is this that makes up the bulk of the one million-plus tonnes of *Oryza sativa* shipped from India to Nigeria.

India and Nigeria have much in common: a colonial past; an extremely ethnically and religiously diverse – and young – population; and, of course, a shared love of rice. It's one reason why the two countries have become key trading partners. As well as rice, Indian-made products, from motorcycles – widely used as taxis in Lagos – to medicines, head to Nigeria. A third of pharmaceuticals in

Nigeria come from India. Going in the opposite direction, and perhaps most important, Nigeria's oil has India as its biggest customer. It's not surprising that the two countries have sought to nurture this bilateral trade relationship. From official visits to trade shows and discussions about sharing skills and investing in infrastructure, there are strenuous efforts on both sides to build a relationship that encourages prosperity.

They're taking on the old money of the West in new ways. Even though that dollar passes through the hands of middlemen, it's an important part of a close relationship between the two nations.

It follows a well-worn path. Wholesalers in Nigeria buy their rice from global traders that buy, sell and transport all kinds of raw foodstuffs, from fats to wheat. These companies are hardly household names but they dictate our diets. The biggest guns are referred to as the 'ABCD' companies: ADM, Bunge, Cargill and (Louis) Dreyfus. They have sophisticated networks of storage and transport facilities, and are involved from field to processing.

They account for a third of the food that crosses borders around the world, and around 75 per cent of the grain trade. This means ABCD products are likely to hit your plate at some point during the day. You can't buy from them, though; they sell to governments, to food-processing plants and multinational producers such as Unilever. There's a massive concentration of economic power in just a few hands. Charities such as Oxfam have claimed this power is used to exploit those at the bottom of the food-processing chain – farmers and labourers – while keeping prices high. The ABCDs might argue that they're at the forefront of pursuing more productive and sustainable forms of agriculture, and future-proofing our food supply.

Their multinational presence means they trade in dollars, the currency of the commodity markets, not nairas or even Indian rupees. The traders hand over the cash, minus their cut, to Indian wholesalers. They in turn convert it to rupees and pay farmers such as Arjun Kumar from the southern Indian state of Karnataka. In 2016, a dollar bought a little over a kilo of rice, but Arjun will never come into contact with that dollar. In fact, he won't receive anywhere near its rupee equivalent.

When we hear about developing economies, Fairtrade and the ethics of trade, much of the debate is about equipping these economies to stand alone. The idea is to lessen dependency on aid, reduce poverty and find ways for people to support themselves within the global economy, because they can't escape from it any more than we can.

India is a fascinating example of how complex the path to development can be. It's also a sleeping giant, a future powerhouse that we'll all – in the West, and in China – be hearing more from.

First and foremost, however a country develops and tries to enrich itself, it needs to ensure that its people are fed. It all starts with agriculture. Growing food sounds simple: plant seeds, water, wait, harvest. Agriculture is referred to as the primary industry but it's a deceptively simple term for a complex process.

Arjun is one of millions of farmers feeding the world. On a small scale, he and his family have to confront the daily challenges of cultivation, of growing and harvesting his crop. On a national scale, farming brings with it the challenges of growing enough for a country to feed its own people. This is known as food security.

Arjun is selling his rice for export, but Indians need to eat too. Cutting down on 'food miles' and sourcing locally has become fashionable in the urban West but there's a more fundamental reason for self-sufficiency: it means countries avoid the risk of outside disruption to their food supply. A well-nourished population is a productive one.

Most countries take food security seriously; in India it became particularly fashionable in the 1960s. While the rest of the world was tuning in and checking out, Indian farmers were experiencing a transformation of their own: the Green Revolution brought higher-yielding species of crops, new farming methods and the use of technology. Like their American counterparts, Indian farmers were focusing on boosting output, although the emphasis was on feeding their own, rather than selling abroad. They even stopped exporting rice when there was a global shortage, and there's a national policy of subsidising food. The pull of the dollar is strong though, of course, and many Indian farmers do export their produce, bringing in valuable foreign income.

India looks, on the face of it, well set. It has the world's largest area under cultivation for wheat and rice, and paddy fields are a common sight across the country. India is also the largest producer of milk, pulses and spices.

Is it fair to assume that the population of a country that produces so much food is well off and well fed? Tell an Indian they look 'prosperous', and the inference is that they're looking . . . curvaceous. This is not considered an insult. Hindu deities tend to be decidedly rotund, such is the national emphasis on eating plenty. Is this then a land flowing with milk and honey, with food to spare? Sadly, as we'll see, it's anything but.

Arjun Kumar's rice harvest may be what's brought the dollar

to India's shores but his is not a lucrative business. Half of India's population relies on agriculture for its income. That's a colossal proportion for a modern economy. But agriculture makes up only one dollar in every six of India's output, its GDP, in any one year. With half of India's workforce working for one-sixth of the country's income, that's a lot of work for very little return.

It's also a fickle, tempestuous business, which means that it's risky for Arjun to rely on farming to earn his rupees. That's not because demand is shaky. Everyone has to eat and as populations grow there are ever more mouths to feed. Demand for food is not simply certain; it's guaranteed to increase. And that demand won't – in fact can't – collapse completely if the price of rice or wheat jumps. People need food, and they need it every day. In other words, the demand for food is fairly 'inelastic', or insensitive to price moves. On the other hand, if the price of a television set shoots up, people hang on to their old ones longer and don't buy a new one. Demand for luxuries is more 'elastic' when it comes to price.

That's a universal truth – whether you live in Delhi, Delaware or Dubai. Those on lower incomes spend a greater proportion of their incomes on food, and therefore might be more likely to cut back if prices soar. In other words, their demand may be slightly more elastic.

The issue for Arjun and millions of farmers like him all over the world is whether they can rely on agriculture for a high enough income whether they can supply enough to make a living at a competitive price.

Rice demands a lot of land and a fair amount of labour – and India has plenty of both – but it is also a very thirsty crop. In a country where irrigation systems are expensive, more than half the rice farmers are at the mercy of rainfall: it's the south-west monsoon Arjun has to worry about, and he's not alone. Two-thirds of the country's land is considered prone to drought, and in India three-quarters of the annual rainfall arrives between June and September. This can work the other way, of course. In 2016, the heaviest monsoons in three years were good not only for umbrella salesmen; they reinvigorated farmers' livelihoods. Across India, weather forecasts – and the first downpours of the year – are as eagerly awaited as the latest Bollywood offering.

Supplying the world with food is a complicated business. As if harvests weren't already volatile enough, India's farmers face many other hurdles. Their farms tend to be tiny, on average less than two hectares. Small wonder, then, that Arjun Kumar may not be able to afford to put in the irrigation systems or invest in the machinery that would make the land more productive. If he could increase the size of his farm or join up with the farmer next door, he'd benefit from the 'economies of scale' and buying a tractor would be far more cost effective. More profit on every kilo of rice.

To pull in more dollars, why can't Arjun Kumar focus on growing his farm to a more effective size? At almost two thousand miles long, India is hardly short of land. But it's not that simple. Red tape – bureaucracy – the scourge of business around the world, features heavily in India. The culture of form-filling and never-ending processes and procedures appears to date back to the time of the Raj. Property rights are complex and confusing; records of who owns what can be hard to come by. There have been endless land reforms but most have acted against the interests of the smallest farmers.

If Arjun manages to overcome these hurdles, he might still fall foul of India's maligned storage and distribution system. About one in three tonnes of the food from farms rots before it's sold.

Substandard warehouses and roads simply can't ensure his rice reaches other parts of the country.

If freight does make it in a fit state to India's ports, they're too limited to process the sheer volume of goods produced in this industrious economy. Add in paperwork and officialdom, and it can take days to clear an item through these ports as opposed to hours in their American counterparts. India may get the dollar, but supplying the pound of rice in return is hard work.

Some of these issues are particularly marked in India, but they highlight the struggle that unites small farmers across developing economies.

Others may face even more fundamental obstacles to growing food, from the wrong terrain and an unfriendly climate to a lack of workers. Many farmers struggle to produce enough to move beyond subsistence level and, even when they do, their size makes them vulnerable. They're at the mercy of global markets, where prices are dictated by larger players with lower costs. Even at home, they may have to compete with cheap imports. In Africa, for example, small farmers face heavily subsidised foodstuffs 'dumped' from Europe. The EU guarantees its farmers prices for sugar, for example, but it restricts imports from Africa.

The Fairtrade movement, which aims to give farmers a fair, sustainable level of income for their produce, sprang up in response to these imbalances across the developing world. In India, it covers a multitude of products and over a million small farmers and workers, but they're in the minority.

Chasing the export dollar is attractive for the government – and Arjun – but it means there might not be enough left to feed India's people. The volatile nature of farming means that agricultural labourers, for example, might not be able to afford to buy what they sow. The government does have a programme of subsidising food but corruption and inefficiency may bump up the price instead.

Agriculture is an old, old industry and, for many, it still means poverty. In order to survive, small independent farmers are being pulled kicking and screaming into the modern global economy. Their products are in great demand but it is not easy to meet that demand. The way the global food trade operates means farmers see little of the spoils. Arjun Kumar's living a game of jeopardy, and even if he can afford to feed his family, any casual labourers he employs may not be able to. And with half the population under the age of twenty-five, they have a lot of mouths to feed. India might be one of world's biggest producers of rice and milk, but it's home to a quarter of the world's malnourished.

As it's so labour intensive, farming absorbs a sizeable proportion of the workforce. But it rarely brings prosperity. Arjun isn't getting rich on his share of that dollar.

Now that China has paused to reflect and reset, and despite the problems facing Arjun, India is in fact the world's fastest-growing big economy. Its GDP, the nation's income, rose by 7 per cent in 2017, although the usual caveats about separating spin from facts in national statistics apply, especially in a country as spread out as India.

To some degree, India can certainly pat itself on the back, and not just about the extra cash it's generating year by year. Children are more likely to survive childhood, and to see their sixty-fifth birthday. They're also more likely to be able to read: over seven out of ten Indians are now literate.

During the nineteenth century, India was the world's second-largest economy, but it then fell behind. Playing catch-up has led India to follow an unorthodox path with unorthodox results. This is partly a result of the legacy left behind by the British Empire, which concentrated on extracting and trading natural resources, including tea and spices, to serve the ruling nation's own needs. There was heavy investment in the services needed to support that trade, ranging from railways to an immense civil service. But other sectors, including manufacturing, were neglected. Independence revealed an economy that was only partially developed and stripped of vast amounts of its wealth. The different economic path the country then took was due partly to India's diverse nature and partly, it must be said, to a lack of planning and government policy. India's unique approach could arguably be seen as the result of accident as well as improvisation.

The West authored what it is viewed as the definitive recipe for success, a clear series of steps towards modernisation and prosperity. Follow the same path as the old money, and every dollar earned can be multiplied several times over. It's a formula that's timeless, and it has easily been adapted around the globe. It lies behind the transformation of China in recent decades and, even more recently, of the likes of Vietnam.

The recipe harks back to the eighteenth century, when the Industrial Revolution turned the old ways of working or, to be precise, farming, upside-down in the UK. In 1960 an American economist called Walter Rostow identified various stages an economy typically goes through to 'develop' – turning the raw ingredients into a finished product. The stages he identified go like this:

1. Traditional society: An agricultural economy based on subsistence farming with little trade. There's a limited supply of basic tools and machinery, meaning workers aren't very efficient and there's not much surplus produced that might be sold elsewhere.

2. Pre-conditions for take-off: Agriculture becomes more mechanised and more output is traded. There's investment in the physical environment, e.g. irrigation systems. Savings and overall investment grow, albeit on a small scale. There's more emphasis on social mobility, development of national identity and shared economic interests. Some external funding may come into play, for example from aid or workers overseas.

3. Take-off: Manufacturing industry assumes greater importance, albeit with a small number of industries (textiles and clothing tend to be at the forefront). Agriculture declines in importance. While it continues to employ the majority of people, many are flocking to cities, in search of the relative riches manufacturing offers. Political and social institutions start to develop, more sources of funds from outside might be needed. Savings and investment become larger scale.

4. Drive to maturity: Industry grows and becomes more diverse, focusing more on producing goods for consumers as well as machinery. There's a rapid development of transportation and social infrastructure (e.g. schools and hospitals). As technology and its use improves, growth and higher incomes spread across the nation.

5. Age of mass consumption: Industry dominates the economy. Output levels grow, enabling increased consumer expenditure – even on luxury items. The growing importance of the middle

class enables the growth of the tertiary or services sectors – from restaurants to hairdressers and beyond.

For Rostow, the recipe stopped there. It encompassed the 'first' Industrial Revolution, the use of water and steam to mechanise production, and the 'second', the use of electricity, to ramp up that production. But to be a fully-fledged 'developed' global economy in the twenty-first century, a few more stages can be added.

These include the expansion of the service sector in response to the growing importance of consumers, until it becomes the larger part of the economy. Then there's making those extra earned dollars work for your country: investing those export earnings, and company profits, in companies and profits abroad, to maximise reach and influence. In the modern age, it's also imperative to get connected, so we see a greater focus on technology and innovation. The 'knowledge economy', the digital age, the 'third' Industrial Revolution – call it what you will, technology has become the trendiest must-have ingredient. Being at the forefront of scientific development and technology means reaping the most rewards – especially as robots threaten to replace the most basic of jobs. And that means being braced for the 'fourth' Industrial Revolution where a fusion of technologies will blur the lines between the physical, digital and biological spheres.

Developing is a painstaking process, the ultimate aims of which are to make your economy more valuable and to grow prosperity, although that can be at the expense of equality. The reasoning is that the finished result should be a whole load more cash than you started with. During the nineteenth century, income in the UK doubled (once inflation is taken into account) thanks to the age of the machine.

Set out like that, it's easy to understand why the average American is sitting on a much larger pile of dollars than, say, the average person in Burkina Faso. That country, one of the poorest on the planet, has barely started: 67 per cent of its people work in agriculture.

What does this say about India and how it's earned its dollar? How typical is Arjun? How far into the recipe has India gone? Many of its fast-growing Asian rivals have made their dollars by drawing on cheap labour and foreign investment to make and sell to the West. That has not been India's way. The fastest-growing major economy hasn't actually gone through the process of building up a large-scale manufacturing industry. It's shied away from the example set by its former colonial masters. In fact, there was little attention paid to establishing manufacturing, or entrepreneurship, during colonial times. There was equally little in the days following independence, when the focus was on the aftermath of partition, and getting this diverse, scattered country to function. Thoughts have only recently turned to firing up India's factories on a global scale.

India still shows little interest in harnessing power abroad. For every dollar India invests overseas, China spends thirty-six. India simply doesn't have the spare cash, the same amount of export earnings and the build-up of reserves. It also may be less inclined to flex its financial power in this way. India has effectively cast aside the traditional recipe and gone off menu. And it's spiced things up.

༄

The *average* Indian's income might have almost tripled since 2000 but that doesn't mean that all Indians are doing well. Arjun still spends his life praying that the rains will come, that his rusty tractor will last the year and that the landlord won't double the rent. One in five Indians, many of them farmers, live on less than $2 per day. Despite overall advances in living standards and education, their children still may not even finish primary school.

Who's enjoying the spoils? Where's this boom in income coming from? Geographically, the answer isn't far away. It lies in the gleaming, hushed corridors of India's new corporate temples, populated by engineers whose qualifications read like a university prospectus.

Bangalore *is* IT. It's the centre of India's information technology revolution. It lies within a hundred miles of Arjun's farm but it might as well be on another planet. Call centres nestle against outsourced technology departments and data-processing plants. They're servicing banks, big companies and clients on the other side of the world in all things technical, from providing IT help desks to developing cutting-edge robotics, and they're finding virtual solutions to issues the world might not yet even know it faces. Welcome to the tech sector, home to India's finest – and richest. Its explosion has created India's own gold rush. In comparison, China's industrial growth looks almost snail-like.

Tata Consultancy Services, for example, took its first offshore client in 1974. By 2005, it employed 45,000 people. In 2017 it employed over 300,000, and is one of the largest companies in India. There are many more companies like Tata, offering IT services, consulting and business solutions, which incorporates all that munching and spewing out of data, at much cheaper rates than firms in the West. The outsourcing of IT departments and call centres to India and the shifting of manufacturing to China happened for the same reason, and caused a similar outcry.

The impact has been extraordinary. India has established itself as the world's technology service centre, prising dollars from corporate hands in dozens of countries. It's a sector that's now worth over $100 billion, compared to just $2 billion twenty-five years ago. Growth across the service sector has varied between 7 to 10 per cent per year over the last decade, several times that of agriculture.

In 2016, high-tech enterprises accounted for almost 8 per cent of India's economy, and created some very rich individuals. Over half of India's wealth belongs to just 1 per cent of its people. Overall, India's economy is more unequal than that of the USA, Russia and even China, according to the World Economic Forum.

Those working in these offices may never have seen a dollar bill or scanned the aisles of Walmart. But the engineers in Bangalore's @Walmartlabs spend their working days worrying about how Lauren Miller can be persuaded to part with her dollar thousands of miles away. They're crunching numbers and information to work out how they can make her shopping trip smoother, more interactive and ultimately more profitable for Walmart. In the retailer's words, 'Walmart #datascientists are cooking up a global data fabric that transforms #bigdata into big insights.' They'll focus on all stages of the shopping 'experience', from the logistics of ordering and getting food to the stores to where it should be placed in-store to get the shopper to make an impulse buy. If there's a sudden heat wave, they'll work out how many ribs should be in the chiller for that impromptu barbecue. Poring over the numbers has enabled supermarkets to work out that new parents are stocking up not only on nappies but also on beer: the new arrival means more nights at home. So they moved the beer fridges. Big data equals big bucks. Indian engineers are intent on the pursuit of the dollar, but these dollars are spent on the other side of the world.

Similar projects are being undertaken in glass and concrete temples across Bangalore, and increasingly other cities too.

Twentieth-century India might have missed out a few steps in the recipe to modernise, skipping over large-scale manufacturing to embrace the technological revolution, but it's manipulated the formula to suit its own needs and tastes, resulting in the economic version of new-wave fusion cuisine, the kind of eclectic fare combining tradition with innovation that's found in the trendiest cafes catering to the new moneyed engineers of Bangalore.

How did India do it? The country has no shortage of young labour – the vast majority are unskilled, but an emphasis on training engineers that dates back to the British Empire, and the growth of India's railways, meant that there was a pool of workers well placed to take up keyboards in the digital revolution. That this revolution happened in Bangalore, 1,350 thousand miles from the capital, Delhi, is no accident either: the new industry was able to escape the beady eye of government and burdensome regulation. Compared to most other Indian cities, Bangalore also has relatively sophisticated infrastructure, which has allowed giants such as Tata Consultancy Services, Wipro and Infosys to flourish.

India has also made a name for itself as an exporter of top-flight engineers. Despite having the entire US population on their doorstep, Silicon Valley's poster children (or teenagers, given their relative age) Google and Microsoft looked to India for their bosses. Microsoft CEO Satya Nadella was born in Hyderabad and graduated in electrical engineering from Maniapal, a specialist tech-incubator. Sundar Pichai, Google's chief, grew up in a two-room apartment in Tamil Nadu before graduating in metallurgical engineering from a specialist university in West Bengal.

Increasingly, there are fewer reasons for the most ambitious to leave India's shores. Bangalore, in particular, is becoming India's Silicon Valley, a ready-made marketplace where enterprising engineers can meet financiers keen to get a slice of India's tech boom. Outside the USA, it's one of the top destinations for venture capitalists looking for the next big digital thing. However, India has yet to rise fully to that challenge. Over the last decade, for example, the growth of ecommerce has seen the emergence of India's own homegrown online retailer, Flipkart, but its value remains dwarfed by Amazon and Alibaba, both of which have tightened their grip on the Indian market.

For now, the outsourcing of routine tech and services remains India's niche. This is an industry that's moving at the speed of fibre-optic broadband. Cloud computing and digital services are changing the way firms see the role of IT in growing their businesses: they want higher value and more innovative services. The big consultancies are investing heavily, but such services need fewer, more specialised staff. India needs to keep up.

At the same time, a pressure to cut costs has coincided with a rise in salaries. Engineers can't be created overnight, and their supply is limited, so staff are starting to demand higher wages. India is no longer quite as cheap as it once was. It's the same story as with manufacturing pay in China, and is a standard by-product of development.

The future of tech in India could look very different and become more sophisticated. The business wasn't labour-intensive to start with, but it could start to employ even fewer people. This could increase inequality in one of the world's most unequal economies. The IT sector accounts for 8 per cent of the economy's value, but those creating that value are punching way above their weight.

According to official figures, tech employs less than 1 per cent of the 460 million-strong workforce. India has a population of 1.3 billion people; one in five of the world's people of working age lives there, and that proportion is rising. The country needs to find an extra million jobs per month just to keep up with its population growth. Yet, since 2016, the tech giants have reined in their hiring plans. A further tweak to India's recipe may yet be needed.

Tech is bringing prosperity to India at a rate of gigahertz, but not to all Indians. It has created a tiny and comparatively super-wealthy new middle class, in a massively underdeveloped country. However, it's not enough to lift Arjun out of poverty and bring India's economy into the premier league. Tech alone can't provide for the masses. India is chasing dollars, and they are certainly flowing in, but it needs to be attracting dollars into industries that provide jobs for a wider section of society.

Sometimes, there's a reason why traditional recipes become timeless classics. They may benefit from the odd tweak but they offer more predictable results. The standard recipe does bring with it inequality, but India's own version may only augment that bitter taste. It still needs more work and, as we'll see, that's under way.

The success of the tech industry shows the strange split personality of India's economy. Bangalore might be at the forefront of tech, but it doesn't reflect the environment in the rest of the country.

Only 15 per cent of households in India are online, says the World Economic Forum. And four out of five of those access the net via a mobile. Being online is largely the preserve of those metropolitan elites who can afford smartphones. Away from urban areas, internet access is scarce to non-existent. That puts India in line with its subcontinental neighbours, but it lags behind the averaging developing country, where two out of five are connected. Why does it matter? The World Bank estimates that doubling internet access to 75 per cent in poorer countries could add $2 trillion on to the world's income, creating over 100 million jobs. Getting online promises more than access to the world of social media or a little light shopping.

Those who are online can struggle to stay connected. Internet speeds can be woeful, thanks to poor digital infrastructure. Only 5 per cent of families have subscribed to broadband. India has the second-biggest smartphone market in the world, but the people who can actually use their phones are in the minority. In total, a billion Indians have mobiles, but dropped calls and patchy network coverage can make them next to useless; they're a status symbol more than a tool of communication.

The introduction of low-cost tech, particularly cheap smartphone handsets, means developing countries are quietly leapfrogging into the modern age. From apps for farmers to online banking, it's the catalyst with the potential to speed up the recipe for success. New markets can be opened up and transactions facilitated in ways that were previously unimaginable.

For Arjun Kumar on his farm out in the sticks, technology could make the difference between thriving or sinking financially. It can mean beating the climate or logistical challenges and getting produce to customers. Of course, such technology costs money, sometimes amounts Arjun doesn't have. But this is a country that developed a $5 smartphone; there is plenty of appetite and know-how within India to recognise and meet the needs of its population. Start-ups in Bangalore, for example, have developed tools to help farmers predict weather changes, forecast crop yields and quality, and take the necessary precautions. They've designed more eco-friendly pesticides, soil additives and more sophisticated machinery to measure and control irrigation levels.

They just need the path ahead clear for them. India's government is trying to modernise, to take advantage of tech for all Indians, not just for the few. In 2015, fresh from hobnobbing with the leaders of Silicon Valley, Prime Minister Narendra Modi unveiled a list of nine targets, including wider WiFi coverage and electronics manufacturing. Minded, perhaps, of the homelands where they got their start, the bosses of Google and Microsoft respectively pledged WiFi for 500 of India's railway stations, and cheap broadband for 500,000 villagers. A welcome boost for some; for others, suspicion that India is once again set to become a colony – a digital colony, that is – of the West. Either way, following through on these initiatives will probably be key to India's future success.

Online platforms now allow farmers and wholesalers to compare and set prices nationwide. The use of digital wallets and payment systems is rising exponentially, and the government wants to help; more efficient transactions could substantially benefit farmers such as Arjun. However, India's not just trying to make life easier for 1.3 billion Indians. It's also trying to shine a light into the darkest corners of the economy, expose its workings, and raise more cash for itself.

To get its hands on the money it needs to help India grow, the government has to know what or who it's taxing, and make sure it gets that money in. For all its history of bureaucracy and paperwork, India has struggled to find its taxpayers and get them to pay up. For every dollar of output, or GDP, generated in India through wages or profits, only 17 cents is paid in tax. That's in line with most developing countries, but it is only half the rate of most of the rich countries India is aiming to compete with. Nearly 50 per cent of Americans paid income tax in 2013, compared with less than 3 per cent of people in India. Incomes for many, particularly farmers, are so low in India that they do not qualify to pay tax – but that's still a tiny proportion.

The problem is cold, hard cash; in this case, not dollars but rupees. Until very recently, more than nine out of every ten rupees changing hands in India did so in the form of cash. That's not just for small purchases, but for large ones too, with wads of 1,000-rupee notes being used to pay for property transactions. Half of Indians don't have bank accounts and 85 per cent are paid in cash for their work. For those in the most far-flung villages, the nearest bank might be hours away. In any case, most businesses aren't set up to accept payments in anything but notes and coins. There are only 25 million credit cards in India, one for every fifty people, and only one ATM for every 5,000 people. It's natural for Arjun to pay for his seeds in cash, from money kept at his home.

Cash exists and is popular for a reason. It's readily accepted and easily accessed, especially if it's kept in a handy drawer. That means it's the most 'liquid' of assets. Wealth held in other forms – from bank accounts to property – is more difficult to access and to spend.

India is unusual in depending on cash far more than its international rivals, including China and the US. It's not necessarily bad news: some argue that it meant India was insulated against the full pain of the global financial crisis in 2008. In other countries, banks that had made excessive loans that couldn't be repaid pulled their economies down. This type of borrowing was far less common in India, with its underdeveloped banking system.

India's reliance on cash is partly due to low-paid rural workers such as Arjun who don't have access to banks, and partly due to the tactics of the higher earners who can use it to escape detection by the tax authorities. As a result, up to three-quarters of India's economy might be flying under the radar. It's the black economy: it doesn't exist; it may include shady deals, including bribery, and it can't be taxed.

How can the authorities clamp down on possibly illegal activity, make sure the economy is out in the open and collect taxes efficiently? For Prime Minister Modi, it was time to employ shock and awe tactics.

In an unscheduled address to the nation on 8 November 2016, he warned his people that 500- and 1,000-rupee notes (worth about $7.50 and $15) would shortly no longer be legal tender; they would be worthless. Anyone holding notes of these denominations had less than two months to deposit them in a bank or a post office. If there was proof of how the money had been acquired, up to 4,000 rupees could be exchanged for notes of other denominations. New 500- and 2,000-rupee notes would be issued. The move rendered more than four out of every five notes in circulation in India potentially invalid – a total of about $220 billion. It was a massive move.

This policy provoked a stampede to the bank. India's finance minister claimed that over $40 billion was deposited in the country's banks in the first four days. Queues were long and fights broke out. The government couldn't print and distribute the new notes fast enough. Financial activity across India was gridlocked. To cope with the lack of cash, the government introduced limits on how much could be withdrawn, and then frequently changed those limits. Confusion and chaos reigned.

There were tales of resulting hardship, from parents who couldn't pay their children's medical bills, sometimes with fatal results, to those who no longer had the means to buy food for their families. Factory lines slowed, as owners couldn't buy the raw materials they needed to manufacture products, or indeed to pay their workers. The announcement coincided with the peak season for weddings, on which the life savings of the happy couple's parents are often lavished. Family festivities were threatened with cancellation and there was national outrage. The Indian government was obliged to change the limits on withdrawal specifically to pay for weddings to an amount of up to 250,000 rupees, about $3,600.

Effectively cancelling most of the cash across the nation didn't just smoke out the tax dodgers and criminals. The pain united India's whole population, from the elite of Bangalore to farmers like Arjun Kumar and, perhaps more pertinently, his wife. Millions of women in India habitually stash away odd bits of cash, hidden in wardrobes or under the mattress. This is a country where women's economic empowerment has gone into reverse in recent years: the UN claims over a third of Indian women were part of the workforce a decade ago – that figure has since fallen to a quarter. Eight in ten don't have a bank account. Modi's actions threatened to take away what little control women had over their finances, rendering their savings meaningless, and leaving many in a desperate situation unless they could bank or exchange their notes by the deadline. But to do so, they needed legal papers and proof of how the money was obtained.

Was the price millions faced for this move worth it? Did it flush out the worst of the racketeers? Jewellers were reportedly working flat out in the hours after the prime minister's speech to meet the soaring demand for gold as tax evaders rushed to convert their cash into the next best thing. They found the price of gold being ratcheted up. But, on the whole, organised criminals were being just that: organised. They were already storing their gains in jewellery, property or other forms of wealth. The corrupt, it's claimed, bribed bank officials to set up phoney bank accounts. They were better equipped than rural housewives to cope with the clampdown on cash. The Indian government reckoned one in every five cancelled banknotes wouldn't qualify for exchange or deposit, meaning a $45 billion crackdown on corruption. In the event, the amount trapped was a small fraction of that amount.

But there has been some impact. Indian officials claim that tax revenue has gone up, a welcome boost for the government's coffers. Almost as quickly as the old banknotes disappeared, digital payments took off. Registrations for e-wallet apps soared. From staff wages to rickshaw fares, online payments have become increasingly popular. Modi's great money experiment might not have cleaned up India's economy, but it's propelled it a little faster towards a more modern financial system.

Demonetisation might not have been only a way to bring in money; it's also proved to be a drastic way of getting this still-developing nation to step up. It's enforcing integration into the modern financial world, something all countries have to achieve if they want to play the global game. Being part of the system, and getting more dollars, means changing behaviour.

∽

Urbanisation is a common ingredient in development. All over the developing world, booming populations are deserting the impoverished countryside for the cities. The challenge is to provide work for all those people when they get there.

Given the hardships they face, it's not hard to see what's inspiring so many from India's countryside – once they have extracted themselves from the byzantine land laws – to head for cities in search of a better life.

The streets of India's cities aren't paved with gold. Slum settlements, defined in the Indian census as 'dwellings unfit for human habitation', now house one in six of India's city inhabitants. That's 65 million people, more than the population of the UK. Unfit these slums certainly are: makeshift and cramped with an inadequate water supply and poor sanitation. The districts are rife with disease, vermin and organised crime. In the last fifteen years, those fleeing the misery of subsistence farming have doubled the slum population.

Those 65 million people are now even less likely to be beneficiaries of foreign dollars than when they were working the land. Where they do have work, slum dwellers tend to work in informal, irregular jobs such as picking up rubbish or taking in sewing. The slums may be an embarrassing eyesore to the authorities, but the people living in them largely fly under the official radar.

As India's cities have boomed, so too, almost on the quiet, has manufacturing. As China can testify, manufacturing can be a good bet when there are plenty of cheap workers available. In fact, according to the national census, 30 million people in India work in manufacturing. This is more than twice as many as in the USA, but they're far less productive than their American counterparts. Apart from those employed by a few large companies, most work in relatively unsophisticated small workshops or factories, with poor supply chains.

The figure of 30 million doesn't take into account the women – and children – subcontracted as, say, seamstresses, working cash in hand in order to keep one step ahead of destitution. The nimble fingers of younger workers are particularly well suited to the hand-embroidered items that the Indian garment industry is known for. With that work sometimes outsourced to home workers, it's hard for even the most ethical retailers to keep tabs on the use of child labour.

India is trying to change this. On a much larger scale, it's trying to employ its population by creating its own manufacturing revolution, with an eye on enticing dollars another, more reliable way.

Prime Minister Modi launched the 'Make in India' initiative in 2014. A Hindu nationalist and a divisive figure, Modi swept to power on the promise of an economic facelift. Big foreign manufacturers – and even homegrown companies – have for years been reluctant to locate in India due to complex laws and restrictions. Modi promised to cut through the regulations, making India a place where it was not just wheat and rice that flourished.

There have been some clear signs of success. Foreign investment surged 40 per cent in the six months after the announcement. Boeing, Ford, Coca-Cola and Isuzu are just some of the global brands setting up or expanding in India. In the northern state of Haryana, Panasonic is to build fridges, while down in Bangalore it's teamed up with Tata to explore robotics. Most of all, Foxconn, maker of the iPhone among other gizmos, has developed a taste for all things Indian. Plans for factories to build mobile handsets are under way, while it's also investing in apps such as messaging service Hike. China's Xiaomi, with two factories, already boasts it can churn out a phone per second in India. These companies are attracted by the cheap labour, and by proximity to that booming middle class.

Does this mean India could soon be stealing Walmart's business from under China's nose? Not quite; the country still has a way to go to pull off this stage of the recipe for growth. It's missing a few key ingredients.

Crucially, it lacks infrastructure: ordinary bricks and mortar, from warehouses to roads and schools. Their absence can hold back the amount of dollars India can earn, whether it's in the rice fields of Karnataka or the workshops of Haryana. Arjun Kumar needs access to transportation and adequate storage facilities to ensure his crops are still in an edible condition when they arrive at market.

Half the country's roads aren't paved at all and are easily damaged by heavy vehicles. Manufacturing is frequently delayed by an inability to get hold of the necessary materials. Some estimates give traffic speeds of a maximum of 40 kph on India's highways. That is on the 'high speed' highways, not in the cities. In the USA, speeds closer to 100 kph are more the norm. Two out of every three tonnes of freight are transported by truck as either the railways don't exist or when they do they aren't up to the job. Does this sound familiar? It's not only trade that Nigeria and India have in common.

As more and more people flock to the cities, congestion has become a way of life. The exploding urban population needs affordable housing, efficient ways to travel and a reliable water and electricity supply at home and at work. Many large manufacturers now rely on their own generators, rather than risk hours of power cuts every day. But it's a costly solution.

The gaps are immense. If India's future is its people, they need decent healthcare and schools for their children to ensure a skilled workforce. Infrastructure doesn't create economies, but it can make them run faster and more smoothly. That in turn will boost the amount Indians can produce – and therefore earn.

None of this is news to India's politicians or business leaders. The Indian government has pledged to connect all 650,000 of its villages by road, and yet it has fallen further and further behind its target of building 25 miles per day. Prime Minister Modi has unveiled plans to pump $1 trillion into roads, railways and airports. Two-thirds of that figure was to come from private sources – because who could resist getting a slice of the world's fastest-growing big economy?

Many foreign investors could, it would seem, and they have their reasons. It can take years before it's known whether an infrastructure project can be completed and its rewards gathered. The overhaul of India's railways, for example, is an arduous process. It's not just the bureaucracy involved in securing contracts and carrying out the work, but the significant likelihood of corruption. Energy or land projects can be complex, opaque and lengthy, and in the end vested interests might outweigh all else. India doesn't have the natural resources – most notably oil – of countries such as Nigeria. Those Nigerian reserves are a magnet for foreign money, overriding all other concerns.

Corruption, real or perceived, can be a big issue for developing countries. The World Economic Forum claims it's the biggest obstacle to getting private money behind modernising India. A potentially lucrative contract could involve backhanders and middlemen. Getting funding from banks is also difficult. The government has relaxed the rules to make it easier for foreign companies to invest, but regulation remains confusing. Then there are the problems of getting conflicts resolved and contracts upheld. Paralysis threatens the most promising ideas.

However, there is the political will to change things and it's being exercised in ever more creative ways. For example, the government has offered to insure foreign companies against risk if they agree to tackle India's highways. Slowly, more foreign money is being invested, but the government itself is still stumping up one-third of the $1 trillion it wants earmarked for buildings, ports, railways and so on. At $350 billion, that works out around $300 per person. The government can afford more now that it has its hands on more of India's cash.

To develop its infrastructure and thus power growth, jobs and incomes, the Indian government needs oil. Its ambitious road-building plan requires vast quantities of bitumen (also known as asphalt), which is made out of heavy crude oil. Nigeria can't provide anywhere near enough oil for this – at least not of the right type, nor at the right price. With Iraqi producers prepared to sell oil at a discount, Iraq has become India's most popular source. Where there is oil, there are dollars. No sooner has the rice wholesaler lodged its dollar with a bank than it has been passed to the Hindustan Petroleum Company, which is sending that dollar on to the oilfields of Iraq.

5

The dark price of black gold

India to Iraq

It might be lonely out in space, as Elton John once sang, but every evening at 6 p.m. Delhi time the astronauts on the International Space Station are treated to a spectacular reminder of home. The lights flicker on across India, anointing its cities with great halos, and highlighting its millions of tiny villages.

You might glimpse a similar sight if you're travelling on one of the many flights that connect the Indian subcontinent to every other part of the world. That flight map, with its thousands of criss-crossing lines, traces the paths of people and ideas and commerce. If we could see their routes, we might imagine a similar map tracing the innumerable transactions that underpin the booming commerce emerging from the subcontinent, from Walmart buying IT support in India to Sri Lanka selling tea to Australia. Those trade routes represent billions of dollars, strengthening relationships and enabling economic activity.

Among the most well-worn paths, for both flights and funds, are those that lead to the Middle East. The countries that make up the region have little in the way of industry and, apart from a few locations, they aren't major tourist destinations. Viewed from the space station, this is a region that's still unlit, still basking in fading sunlight while the lamps flicker on in India. It is, however, largely responsible for keeping the subcontinent burning bright. It's oil, not camel safaris or dates, that is the Middle East's key attraction.

To connect its 650,000 villages, India has to pave its new roads with gold – black gold. The Missan oilfields lie some hundred miles north of the southern Iraqi city of Basra, towards the border with Iran. They look like any other desert: boring and barren. For many years this land was the preserve of peasant farmers, eking a living from the dusty terrain. That all changed when the bubbling brook of liquid fuel beneath its surface was discovered in 1975. The Iraqi state took control and invited big foreign companies to operate the oilfields. Cows may still graze in neighbouring plots, but many farmers were pushed aside, and in their place came oil executives from China and Turkey. So widespread was the displacement that the Missan Oil Company has a special compensation committee. In a PR exercise, some locals were offered jobs – guarding the oilfields, for example. Security is not taken lightly; after all, this lucrative land lies close to a disputed border with a fractious neighbour.

For any nation, the discovery of oilfields promises a windfall not just of dollars, but also of power. Hence the label 'black gold'. Having resources on your doorstep can also bring turmoil and volatility. Black gold may be a bountiful blessing; it can also be a curse.

That's not true just for oil barons and their compatriots. Few of us could carry out our daily lives without oil, but that dependency can also weigh on us. We might wonder why our petrol price can escalate so quickly, yet never fall as fast. Or why our government is so keen to wage war in some countries, but ignore other conflicts?

The answers often lie in the workings of the oil sector. It's not simple. Upstream, downstream, derricks and sheerlegs . . . even the language of the industry seems designed to confound. But it is worth trying to understand it. Our journey is about to take us into one of the most fascinating and universally relevant facets of how our world works.

∽

To drill down into the oil story, it's time to go fossil hunting. Crude oil is a key component of highway surfaces as well as countless other everyday items, from chemicals to plastic bottles. This rich, foul broth, made up of a blend of mud-coated rotting animal and plant matter bubbling away for millennia in the nooks between sedimentary rocks, is the fuel that keeps the wheels turning on roads across the globe. Hand in hand with the dollar, it also keeps many economies going.

Being able to lavish dollars on oil is a route to prosperity, as India well knows. To satisfy surging demand, India's roadbuilders need bitumen, which is ordered from a supplier, who needs to get it from a processing plant, which means knocking on the door of the government-controlled Hindustan Petroleum Company. HPC refines over 16 million metric tonnes of oil per year, which is transported across the country via over 300 km of pipelines. Our dollar was exchanged into rupees at a bank by the rice wholesaler. The bank can then sell the dollar on to HPC. One of its refineries will use its dollars to enable it to buy a barrel of oil from Iraq.

The various uses of oil have been in evidence for many centuries. Traces have been found in the pyramids of ancient Egypt and in the tar used to seal the wrappings of the mummies entombed there. The Latin word 'petroleum', literally 'rock oil', first appeared in the sixteenth century. It was an apt description: until the nineteenth century, crude was largely skimmed off the seepages from rocks, or oil slicks. Lamps in the 1800s relied chiefly on whale oil but that changed around 1850 when Canadian geologist Abraham Gesner distilled a new fuel, kerosene, from petroleum; this proved cheaper and cleaner than whale oil – and its discovery helped save the whale.

The rapid march of industrialisation prompted a huge thirst for oil. Around the same time, large crude reserves were discovered in Titusville in the American state of Pennsylvania. The first large-scale commercial oilfield, Spindletop, went on stream in 1901, at a time when the combustion engine, which gave birth to the aircraft and the motorcar, was coming into wider use. Oil was crucial in the birth of the modern era, and it has since taken over the world.

'Crude oil' is a catch-all label covering a variety of grades of oil extracted from the ground or from below the seabed. It varies in density, consistency and toxicity. Despite the 'black gold' label, it comes in many shades, from the darkest black to a pale yellow. The lightest oil flows well, is easy to get out of the ground, and evaporates quickly. The lighter it is, potentially the less harmful it is too. The heaviest is typically the most sludge-like and the hardest to pump; it's the most toxic to the environment and likely to coat sea birds' feathers when spilt.

Today, the gasoline lapped up by thirsty cars and jets comes from the most refined: the light distillates. 'Light' may imply – as when 'lite' is attached to certain drink brands – something that's not quite the real deal. Applied to oil, 'light' signifies a purer material. The less-polished medium grades are used to make plastics and chemicals, fuel ships and power stations, and heat homes.

The roughest oil is perfect for bitumen; hence the Indian government's interest.

India's dollar is chasing Basra Heavy, a discount crude oil sold to buyers who want a budget alternative to the premium Basra Light. Despite having oil reserves in the Bay of Bengal and the state of Rajasthan, India has to look abroad to keep its wheels turning. Typically, Iraq sells India up to a million barrels of oil per day, with Basra Heavy in one in five barrels.

This is a run-of-the-mill transaction in the life of the global economy. Almost a hundred million barrels of medium-grade oil are currently consumed around the world every day. That's the equivalent of over two litres of crude oil per day for every man, woman and child, without taking into account other forms of energy use.

Usage varies widely. Unsurprisingly, by *total* oil consumption, the USA comes in top: the average American gets through about 10 litres of oil or oil products per day. This is due partly to its road-tripping gas-guzzlers – total energy use peaks over the summer driving season – and its harsh winters, when the biting cold gets north-easterners cranking up the heating. Next comes China with its chugging factories. Vying for third place are India and Japan, while Russia completes the top five. Between them, these countries use 40 million barrels a day according to the Energy Information Administration. (None of them, however, actually has the highest oil consumption per head. Small islands such as Singapore tend to have that distinction: small population, huge shipping industry.)

Buying a lot of oil is a sign of a growing economy, and India and other developing nations are leading the charge: global consumption has been increasing on average by around 1–2 per cent, or one million barrels per day, since 2010, as industrial activity picks up in countries such as China – whose populations are spending their newly acquired wealth on cars. The global financial crisis and China's slowdown have led to the demand for oil being 'hit'. This does not mean that demand is going into reverse but that the pace of growth is slower.

While China is slowing down, other countries are booming. India provides an insight into the potential for future demand. Even with all its ambitious road-building programmes, oil consumption is still the equivalent of about half a litre a day per person: one-twentieth of the average American's. That could change very rapidly once those roads are finished and if India starts realising more of its economic potential. The International Energy Agency predicts India will be the fastest-growing user of oil over the next two decades. Whether its needs can be met is another question.

The top five producers of oil vary each year, but Russia and the USA usually feature in the list. So too do Saudi Arabia, Iran and Iraq. There's a mismatch between those who supply and those who buy. Some countries are chasing after the resources of others. This means the thirst for oil has led to special relationships, cliques, rivalries and even bloodshed. The price of oil is not only financial.

The unit by which oil is measured has its roots in medieval England. The 'barrel', equivalent to 42 gallons or 159 litres, refers to a 'tierce', an old English vessel for holding wine. These days the oil will be in tankers rather than in actual barrels, just as wine is now sold in bottles. And in the twenty-first century, a dollar doesn't buy much of a barrel.

Putting a price tag on that 'barrel' of oil is harder than it sounds. This is a major issue. If India is buying a million barrels a day and is building 20 km of roads per day, a few dollars one way or the other makes a massive difference. So how is it sold, and what does it cost? This is where some of the strange and complicated mechanisms of the global economy come to light.

Just as crude oil refers to a range of products, there's no one single 'oil price', despite what headline writers might imply. Each grade from each region comes with its own price tag. When journalists talk about the oil price, typically they mean one key measure: Brent blend, the light oil from the North Sea oilfields. It gets so much attention because it's the most desirable type: easily refined into petrol and, as it's pumped out of the sea, easily transported to the other side of the world. The price of Brent Crude is used as a type of shorthand for the general oil price, as it's simpler than calculating the average price of all the different types of oil globally, especially as those prices are constantly changing.

Prices are arrived at by the process of trading, buying and selling. Whatever form markets take, from the gleaming dealing rooms of American banks to the dusty alleys of Iraqi souks, they all operate on the same principle: bringing together buyers and sellers and deciding a price that matches demand with supply. Pick up a pomegranate in Baghdad's souk, and its price will reflect not only the cost of producing it – the effect of weather on the harvest, the price of transport and pesticides, etc. – but also how much buyers want it. If demand is high the producer might be able to increase the price and make a bigger profit. On the other hand, if it's been a bumper crop, and it's a quiet day in the souk, prices can fall as the seller tries to offload stock. The aim is for the stall to have sold out by the end of the day and to have taken as much cash as possible.

Similarly, oil producers want to maximise their profits, but agreeing a price with them takes a lot more than simply turning up at the oilfield with a fistful of dollars for a quick bartering session. Buyers and sellers are scattered across the globe, and their needs – like the grades of oil on offer – are diverse. The complexity of extracting and processing oil creates complexity for both buyer and seller. Oil needs to be transported internationally through a network of tankers and pipelines. The typical buyer will want to acquire a number of barrels, and will need to arrange storage for them.

A lot of infrastructure and a lot of forward planning are involved in buying oil. Generally, buyers will be planning so far in advance that they'll need to know how much oil they're going to buy months down the line, and what the cost will be. Buyers and sellers have come up with an ingenious way of being able to plan ahead: a 'futures contract', which is essentially a promise to trade a particular quantity of oil at a particular price at a particular point in the future. This contract means the buyer – in this case, HPC – is obliged to buy the barrel of oil at a fixed price on a fixed date (typically three months ahead), and the seller, usually an oil producer, is obliged to sell it at that price on that date.

On the whole, buying direct in this globalised age isn't an option. A centralised market, staffed by professional traders, is the norm. It is commodities traders, many thousands of miles away, who'll broker the deal and determine how many dollars India has to part with to buy the barrel of oil to pave its road. The contract itself is just a piece of paper, and it might even be bought by HPC, via a trader, from another customer. HPC would then have the right to buy the oil at the price agreed by that contract a few months down the line.

As if the issues of supply and demand weren't enough, there are two added elements in play here: sentiment and speculation.

A lot of that comes down to the role of the middlemen. Commodity traders are effectively upscale market traders, which is why they're sometimes referred to as 'barrow boys and girls'. They trade in anything that's mined, extracted or farmed, including energy, metals and food. They're as old as civilisation itself. Originally, they'd have traded livestock, priced in gold or silver. As markets expanded internationally and products became more complex and sophisticated, so too did the way the traders functioned. It was Amsterdam's stock exchange that was the first to evolve into a commodities marketplace, but it's the Chicago Board of Trade that's often cited as the first major 'official' futures exchange. Launched in 1864, well before the large-scale extraction of oil, it dealt in wheat, corn, cattle and pigs. Commodities trading used to happen by 'open outcry' – haggling in 'pits' on the trading floor – and traders were instantly identifiable by their garish jackets. Technology saw that off, and transactions now happen electronically; orders are entered remotely and matched by computers.

Analysts and traders still need to know every last detail about their product and the market. Their decisions and actions keep wheels turning and factories churning. They pore over weekly reports from various energy bodies worldwide to find out how many barrels are sitting around – that is, the stocks – and glean an idea of how well supply and demand are matched. They'll review production and also look at current events and trends that might affect supply in the coming months; for example, whether companies in Nigeria are being squeezed by insurgency. On the demand side, for instance, are Chinese factories slowing down and consuming less? Those are examples of the 'fundamentals' that help determine how many dollars a barrel of oil *should* cost, based on all the available evidence.

The traders will also be using their gut instinct about future risks. Are they concerned about disruption to supply in Nigeria? Outbreaks of unrest in the Gulf region? Is there a risk China's factories could perhaps halt production? Their instincts might be based on intuition, rumour or bar-room gossip. All this comes under the heading of *market sentiment*. Gloomy or upbeat, those hunches can make many dollars' difference to the cost of the barrel India is after.

Above that is *speculation*. Sentiment is blending heart and head when it comes to making an informed decision about the future direction of the oil market. Speculation is acting on it, not out of a desire to buy or sell oil, but in order to make money from the transaction. Speculators don't actually take delivery of or dispatch barrels of oil; they simply bet on whether they expect oil prices to rise or fall by buying and selling those futures contracts. When speculators feel optimistic about the price, they buy more oil, even if they aren't actually going to take possession of it. They can sell that contract on to someone else at a profit. Get it right, and pocket the cash. It's no different from the way many investors treat shares in the stock market.

The oil game is big business. According to one commodities exchange, actual barrels of oil are traded in fewer than 5 per cent of the thousands of transactions the traders see flowing into the computerised systems every minute. The piece of paper HPC buys might have come from someone with no intention of ever actually buying oil; they just wanted to sell that piece of paper on to HPC and make a profit. Traders will offer contracts for each type of oil. If they can see there's overwhelming demand, they'll push the price up. The opposite happens when demand is weak or there's a glut. Speculation can push the market price away from what the fundamental supply and demand suggest should be a rational figure. It's punters having a flutter on the most coveted commodity around and distorting the market.

Speculation can strongly influence the oil price. In fact, it can cause huge swings in the price and create great uncertainty. It's speculators on the other side of the globe who dictate how much India pays for bitumen, or if it can even afford to build its roads. They dictate how much Americans spend on petrol. Ultimately, they impact on fortunes and the pattern of power around the globe.

It might seem mad, or at least grossly unfair, but speculation is such a profitable part of the modern finance industry that there's little incentive to crack down on it. It's not in the interest of the moneymen to do so. Individual governments might feel frustrated but in the age of global, interconnected markets they are powerless to act alone. Doing away with futures contracts wouldn't help, either. They're the lifeblood of factories, shipping companies, airlines, petrol suppliers – and ultimately to nations.

It's reasonable to wonder if there is some other way of controlling the price of oil. This is where OPEC, or the Organization of the Petroleum Exporting Countries, comes in. Set up in 1960 in Baghdad, only 300 miles down the road from Basra, OPEC is made up of just twelve countries: from the oil baron Persian Gulf States of Saudi Arabia, Iraq, Iran and Kuwait, through major African producers such as Nigeria and Angola, to relative tiddlers including Ecuador and Equatorial Guinea. Together, they produce around four out of every ten barrels of oil in the world, and six out of every ten that are then exported.

OPEC is more than a cosy support network for like-minded countries. It exists to 'coordinate and unify the petroleum policies of its member countries and ensure the stabilisation of oil markets, in order to secure an efficient, economic and regular supply of petroleum to consumers, a steady income to producers, and a fair return on capital for those investing in the petroleum industry'. Or, in the words of its critics, it's a cartel, a group that exists to influence oil prices to protect its own profits and interests.

OPEC is supposed to meet regularly to coordinate production, thus keeping the oil price steady and delivering certainty and stability for its members. It does this mainly by trying to fix supply, as limiting supply should push the price higher. It sets 'production targets', which might mean ordering members to turn down the flow of oil to bolster prices when they're low, and members are meant to agree to quotas and restrictions. But it doesn't always work. In theory, as its largest member, Saudi Arabia dominates and should control OPEC, but the others are, on the whole, each significant enough to make a mark. Any individual member might decide to be selfish and ignore a pledge to cut output, something that's even more likely if it suspects another member is doing the same. Since 1980, the vast majority of OPEC production quotas have been breached. In such a diverse and geographically spread group, suspicions, tensions and incentives to cheat are high.

OPEC's power has diminished with the growth of operations in the USA and Russia. Yet OPEC remains a key player; it even has its own oil price, the OPEC Basket. Together, its members produce about four times as much crude oil as the USA does every year. Traders will still take into account what OPEC is saying and doing when they're trying to put a value on a barrel of oil.

Setting the price of one of the most important and sought-after products in the world is a complex and fickle business. This is nothing new; the oil price has, for a variety of reasons, experienced sharp highs and lows for as long as it's been in common use.

In the early 1860s, the American Civil War was a factor in causing the oil price to jump sharply. Since then, it's easy to see how changing fundamentals – American car ownership taking off in the 1920s, the Suez Canal crisis, or the Great Depression – have caused bumps and troughs along the way. For the most part, however, from 1960 to the early 1970s the oil price trundled along at between the equivalent of $20 and $40 per barrel in today's money. If India had pursued its road-building programme a hundred years ago, it would have been pretty confident of how much oil it was likely to get for its buck.

But with the 1970s came change – both geopolitical, and to the workings of the market – and for the oil price that has spelt massive swings, a vertiginous, head-spinning rollercoaster ride. Since then, the price per barrel has dropped below $4 and it's also spiked above $120. On the face of it, that's a thirtyfold increase. Of course, the standard cost of living has risen over time, too, but strip that out and the rise is more like six-fold, which is still dramatic. This is something that affects every country – and every person – on the planet.

The power base of the world economy shifted emphatically in the middle of the twentieth century, with the explosion in car ownership and rise of OPEC. The biggest oil producers, such as Saudi Arabia, found themselves courted by the energy-hungry West, with the mutterings of their officials pored over by traders as prices inched higher from the 1960s onwards. Then, in 1973, Arab oil producers boycotted America and punished the West in response to its support for Israel in the Yom Kippur War against Egypt. That made the oil price quadruple in 1973–4. It gave immense power to OPEC, and great weight to the slightest murmurs of its members. It made the King of Saudi Arabia extremely wealthy.

At that time, following the Bretton Woods agreement, which aimed to ensure global financial stability by making the dollar the backbone of the global economy, the greenback was the unit of international trade, widely available, and backed by gold. But there was not enough gold being mined to keep up with the number of dollars in circulation. The Bretton Woods agreement collapsed and the dollar's position and reputation were in jeopardy.

To help re-establish the dollar's global credibility, the USA made a deal with Saudi Arabia in 1973 to price and trade all petroleum products in dollars. So the dollar held on to its leading role in commerce, and its value was supported by the insatiable thirst for hydrocarbons. As the whole world needs oil, the dollar was in high demand. In return, the Saudis got America's influence and backing to maintain security, particularly in holding Iran and Iraq at bay – a valuable development for them in such a volatile region.

Reliance on those dollars has meant that oil producers should be more likely to comply with US foreign policy – or at least less likely to retaliate in any disagreement. That, as conflicts with oil producers has shown, hasn't always held true, but oil exporters do ultimately need dollars to remain strong. The whole arrangement has been to the USA's advantage.

With the oil price rising sharply, the earnings amassed by oil-producing countries grew rapidly. This wealth fast became known as 'petrodollars'. Over time, petrodollars have been invested in increasingly sophisticated ways by the governments of those countries. This has included sending dollars back to the USA, by buying bonds and the like, just as China has done recently with its own dollars.

Governments around the world realised that they were going to need a constant supply of dollars if they wanted to purchase oil.

They were therefore more likely to try to align their own currencies with the value of the dollar, to try to avoid being hit with huge and unpredictable costs. They did not want to find the bill for the same quantity of oil doubling overnight as the dollar increased in value.

For the likes of Iraq and India, countries whose friendship and trading relationship goes back centuries, the pricing of oil in dollars makes the whole process cumbersome. While the Hindustan Petroleum Company is buying barrels of Basra Heavy, Iraq is importing rice, tractors and medicines from India. Without the involvement of oil and the omnipotence of the dollar, trade between the two could be about exchanging dinar for rupees. Each extra dollar added to the price of a barrel of oil has a major and far-reaching impact.

Not surprisingly, this situation has frustrated many oil producers and buyers, who resented the USA flexing its muscle this way. Some, including Venezuela and Iran, have looked to sign deals to trade oil in their own currencies. Every so often, there's a restless outcry about pricing oil in other ways. But for the most part the dollar maintains its stranglehold over the oil market, not least as it has the support of major players and makes trading simpler for the oil markets.

Those geopolitical changes in the wake of the Yom Kippur War were followed in the 1970s and the 1980s by the freeing up of money markets, a liberalisation that encouraged big banks and other investors to think of the oil price as something to gamble on. The birth of the energy futures market in 1978 gave those speculators even more opportunity to make a killing. Those contracts were traded on NYMEX – the New York Mercantile Exchange – which had been originally established to trade butter and cheese a century before. Its purpose then was to bring some unity and stability to dairy prices. Now it served as a platform to allow businesses to insure against wild swings in the oil price, by buying ahead. But it also gave speculators a chance to make a quick profit. So, not only was the whole world relying on the dollar's value for essential energy, the oil price itself was extremely volatile. That's an awful lot of uncertainty to manage, and it's no surprise that most countries want to have as much control over their energy supply as possible.

This anxiety has had an effect on foreign policies and diplomacy around the globe. As China has courted Nigeria for its oil, the USA and its allies have had to maintain a close relationship with the Saudis. That's led to the perception that the West has turned a blind eye to Saudi Arabia's controversial human rights record. Being the kind of record that incurs harsh criticism elsewhere, that's also meant accusations of hypocrisy.

Since the end of the Cold War with Russia, the USA has also been involved in two wars in Iraq, one in Afghanistan and one in Libya. The burning oilfields of Kuwait flashed across television screens in 1991; a little over a decade later, the allies were back, ostensibly smoking out Saddam Hussein's stash of weapons of mass destruction, but it was no coincidence that these hostilities were playing out among the region's vast oil reserves. The war in Afghanistan might have been a response to the Al-Qaeda atrocities of 9/11, but it was also about securing an important pipeline.

These conflicts gave the USA a chance to prove to the world it was the policeman of the global 'petropolis'. It was also protecting its own interests. Having willing partners in the Middle East who can supply oil and production contracts to its companies has been key to America's – and the dollar's – continued dominance of the global economy. It's literally kept the home fires burning, ensured jobs for American oil workers, and cemented demand for the dollar.

⚬⚭⚬

For all involved, oil is both a blessing and a curse. To some degree, we are all at the mercy of changes in the dollar exchange rate and the price of a barrel as determined by global markets. Changes to either have a knock-on effect throughout the economy, something that affects us all.

Oil helps to power hungry importers such as India on a path to economic growth but it also leaves them vulnerable. When the oil price rises, the Hindustan Petroleum Company has to pay out dollars more for each mile of highway India wants to build. That means the government has to find more funds, raising more from taxpayers if it wants its project to stay on the road. Indians would have to pay more to drive on those roads because the price of petrol would rise too. The poorest households would suffer most as they spend a bigger proportion of their earnings on fuel. Restaurants and shops would feel the pinch as richer customers across the country would have less spare cash. To compound the challenge, fuel costs for factories, offices and shops would go up, so they might be forced to push up the prices of the goods and services they sell. For all the government's meticulous planning, it's changes in things beyond its control – the oil price or the value of the dollar – that can leave a lasting imprint on India's prosperity. The same is true all over the world.

In many countries, however, the extremes of the oil prices now have less impact than they once did. In the West, the quadrupling of oil prices in the early 1970s squeezed customers' finances hard. Queues at petrol stations grew as oil prices soared. Prices for everyday items jumped by over one-fifth in some countries, including the UK. Trade unions demanded wage rises to match;

factories couldn't afford to continue production. A global recession ensued.

The further jump in the oil price in 1979, with the Iran–Iraq War, also knocked the wind out of the sails of growth around the world, as did a rise in reaction to the First Gulf War in 1990. What was apparent was that prices and related economic activity in oil-guzzling countries reacted far more violently and quickly to jumps in the oil price than to falls. For most of us, our main exposure to the oil market is through our petrol tanks, and the cost of oil is only one component of the cost of petrol. Most of the money we pay for a litre goes to governments in the form of taxes; some goes towards refinery costs, and so on. Only a couple of cents per litre goes to the petrol station itself. Lower oil prices mean lower profits for oil companies and refiners, so they try to cling on to every last cent for as long as they can, which results in prices tending to fall more slowly than they rise. Given all the factors involved, the price we pay for petrol doesn't precisely mirror the fluctuations in the price of oil.

However, as prices jumped once more at the start of the 2010s, to levels equivalent to those in the 1970s, the reaction on the whole was far more muted. The oil shocks of the 1970s forced a change in behaviour, a building-up of resilience. The West took a long, hard look at how it used oil. Many Western countries are no longer the industrial power-guzzling nations they once were. Factories and cars have become far more energy efficient, which has insulated companies and drivers against some of the increases in oil prices. The biggest economies are now more likely to rely on services for their incomes; banks, for example, don't need oil in the way that industry does. While factories are hostage to higher oil prices, powerless to do anything but to sit and wait for higher costs to hit, speculators on financial trading floors are able to make money out of the volatility of fuel prices. In contrast, concerns over the impact of higher crude prices on growth in India or China remain huge, due to their reliance on the manufacturing industries.

Oil now has less of a stronghold on the energy market, too. Perhaps high costs rather than concerns about climate change and pollution directed research and investment into the quest for mainstream alternative energy sources. Now, there's enough energy provided by hydroelectric sources – dams, essentially – to power economies equivalent to the combined size of Japan, Germany and the UK.

Renewables aren't just a rich country's game. Even India, as it pushes forward with its ambitious highways to prosperity, is looking to make all new cars electric by 2030. Admittedly, much of that electricity will come from fossil fuels, but the International Energy Agency estimates that 23 per cent of electricity now comes from renewable sources. Overall, about 13 per cent of our total energy comes from such sources – and that amount is predicted to triple by 2040. Even though it would mean over 60 per cent still coming from the 'old' fossil fuels, it represents fantastic progress. It's a massive change on just a few decades ago, and even greater change is on the way. With the developing world ratcheting up its fuel demands, it can't come soon enough.

Due to higher oil prices, it has also made more sense for some countries to tap into oil reserves that were too costly to exploit before, such as the UK's North Sea oilfields, the oil locked away under Rajasthan or the shale reserves of Texas. Using what's in our own backyard has become a more attractive and viable option. Extracting oil from shale rock became profitable – and therefore possible – only when oil prices hit over $95 a barrel in the USA. Oil from this source has gone from a trickle to a steady stream in recent years. By 2015, the USA was churning out 5 million barrels per day from shale, meaning it made up more than half of America's oil production. The development of better technology and more efficient extraction means the cost of exploiting shale reserves has been slashed. For the first time for years, the USA briefly produced more oil in 2016 than it imported. Its quest to reduce its reliance on foreign energy is paying off. Some estimates now put America's oil reserves ahead of Saudi Arabia's and Russia's.

The heart of the matter is energy security, insulating the economy from shocks to the energy market with regard to either price or supply. This also means focusing on fuel supply chains, including the generation, transmission and distribution of electricity. The ultimate goal is for the home of the dollar no longer to feel that it can be held to ransom by the oil barons of the Middle East. This situation has been labelled by the *Economist* magazine 'Sheikh versus Shale'. The shift in oil reserves may lead to a shift in dollars and power, and a redraft of the geopolitical map in America's favour. Eventually, if and when the world becomes less dependent on oil, the dollar's dominance will come under threat. But the development of shale has, to some extent, pushed that day just a little further away.

Future supply could be a far greater issue. There's only so much oil buried beneath the ground, and fewer new oilfields, most of them quite small, are being discovered. Expert opinions differ, but some claim that the rate of production may hit a high – 'peak oil' – over the next couple of decades. Analysts at HSBC believe that by 2040, the world may be several million barrels a day short of what it wants to consume, unless more can be produced. That's the equivalent of four Saudi Arabias' worth. Just imagine what that will do to the price of oil. The rise in renewables might not be able to compensate fast enough. It's a race against time to keep the world's lights on, and its bills down.

∽

Oil still promises immense riches, of course. It particularly benefits state-owned Saudi Aramco, which is thought to be worth some $2 trillion. That would make it a more valuable company than Apple or Google's parent company, Alphabet. Even with the swings in the oil price, old industry is still outperforming new.

Copious oil reserves do offer the prospect of great wealth, but they can leave a country vulnerable, and a drop in oil prices can be extremely painful for the big oil earners. Close to half of Saudi Arabia's annual GDP comes from oil. For decades, awash with petrodollars, Saudi embarked on lavish public-spending programmes. Now, to keep the books balanced, the Saudi government needs oil to maintain a high price.

In 2014, the global oil price fell due to the vast amount being pumped out by Saudi Arabia relative to the faltering demand from China, and fears that that demand could fall even further. As the price dropped, government spending in Saudi had to be cut back for the first time in almost fifteen years. Together with its OPEC colleagues, Saudi agreed to cut output by nearly one out of every twenty barrels it produced in 2017. It was an unusual move but one that stressed the desperateness of the financial conundrum Saudi was facing.

Iraq, too, needs to keep a firm grip on every dollar it makes from selling oil. In 2014, almost of all of its export earnings came from oil. A country relying heavily on a single commodity in this way is known as an economic monoculture. The oil sector accounted for almost half of the country's GDP and funded much of the activity elsewhere in the economy. A drop in the oil price can cause hardship all round.

That's not the only problem faced by Iraq. The curse of black gold has become so widespread that it's got other names: the 'paradox of plenty' or the 'resource curse'. The sad truth is that countries with an abundance of certain natural resources, such as oil, tend to have less economic growth, less democracy and poorer advances in standards of living than countries with fewer resources.

These countries also face economic and political instability. Countries that depend heavily on oil for their income aren't referred to as having a monoculture for nothing: oil interests tend to be overrepresented, in terms of property rights, regulations and power. Inequality is likely to be pronounced, as there's an inevitable gulf in income between those involved in the oil industry and the rest. Swings in prices can bring sharp changes in income, unemployment and civil unrest. In Venezuela, the drop in the oil price in 2014 brought with it rationing, economic disarray and food riots.

Striking oil or gas can also cause economic ripples far from the wells. 'Dutch disease' isn't a virus suffered by livestock or plants; it refers to what happened in the Netherlands after the discovery of gas reserves there in 1959. As its dollar export earnings shot up in the early 1970s, demand for the Dutch guilder, its currency at the time, shot up, too, along with its value. Unlike China and Nigeria, the Netherlands allowed its currency to respond freely to changing demand, and Dutch farmers and factory owners paid the price; their exports became too expensive to compete abroad. Unemployment in the country more than quadrupled between 1971 and 1977.

Investment dropped, causing lasting scars in the parts of the nation that weren't tied up in producing oil or gas.

With everyone chasing the world's favourite commodity, these countries are also more prone to conflict. A country rich in natural resources can become a target for invasion. It was a quest to control Kuwait's oil that led Saddam Hussein to invade in 1990. The USA's interest in Iraq also goes beyond the humanitarian, as American companies, including the giant Halliburton, have benefited from oil contracts in Iraq. In 2014, Iraq again found itself the target of those with designs on its reserves when it came under attack not just from the falling oil price but also from Islamic State (IS).

Without oil, Iraq is hardly a lucrative prospect; its only other major production industry is cement. Even with hydrocarbons, average income per head in Iraq is less than one-tenth of the American figure. The typical Iraqi is just nineteen, and half of adults didn't make it to secondary school. That just emphasises the disruption the country has seen, given that before 1990 Iraq's education system was considered world class. Vast swathes of land are given over to farming, yet food has to be imported in bulk. Conflict has held Iraq back; already vulnerable, it was a soft target, and IS knew it.

The terror group swept through the north and west of the country, seizing the Iraqi oilfields, with a total capacity of nearly 60,000 barrels a day. Although it did not manage to reach the fields of Basra in the south, the impact was still massive. Some estimates say IS was able to make $700,000 per day from selling the oil it seized into Syria or Iran or to makeshift refineries. That money – along with income from selling the antiquities and properties it looted and ransoms from kidnappings – gave IS the ominous distinction of being the best-funded terror group in the world. The money allowed it to recruit, arm and pay fighters in the region and elsewhere.

The price for Iraq wasn't just lost oil money but a full-scale humanitarian crisis. IS's territorial gains were accompanied by war crimes including mass killings, rape and abduction. Almost 3 million Iraqis have been displaced and 10 million were judged to be in need of aid by the UN. The starving citizens of the besieged city of Fallujah, who were subject to shocking atrocities and who saw their homes and roads destroyed, paid a heavy price for IS's thirst for black gold.

A US-led coalition launched airstrikes on IS targets, including its oil operations, and the extremists' grip on the oilfields was loosened as they were forced into retreat. By mid-2017, the military focus was on recapturing the last IS stronghold: the city of Mosul. To equip those fighting IS on the ground – Iraqi troops and Kurdish Peshmerga militia – the Iraqi government had to draw on its oil funds. To defend its people and its oil industry, it has to spend its dollar from the Hindustan Petroleum Company. HPC hands it over to Iraq's state-operated oil company. From there it enters the government's coffers, where it is used to pay for defence.

Iraq has had a long-running relationship with Russia, and in 2014 its ally announced that it stood ready to provide Iraq with weapons to fight terrorism. In its hour of need, that's where Iraq is turning – and sending its dollar. The dollar is moving from oil to guns.

6

Funding the means of destruction

Iraq to Russia

The factory in Izhevsk stretches as far as the eye can see, the buzz of activity a familiar sound in the city since the early nineteenth century. Workers assemble and test military rifles, shotguns and hunting rifles. Their parents may well have done similar jobs, the strict rules of the Soviet Union then dictating exactly how many weapons were to be made – and how – to suit the military requirement. That's no longer the case, and in fact factories like this are busier than ever, now kept open by the demands not of the Kremlin but of the dollar.

Exploiting Russia's assets following the collapse of the Soviet Union, our arms manufacturer – let's call him Dmitry Sokolov – is part owner of a company that makes the equipment for which Russia has become renowned. He's fictional, of course, but for the purposes of our story he represents those making use of the country's assets following the collapse of the Soviet Union. From anti-aircraft guns to tanks to MiG fighters, Russian arms dealers can supply it all. At this point, in the swap between oil and guns, the dollar has a foot in each of the two most controversial areas of the global economy. In 2012, rebuilding its military, Iraq spent $4.2 billion on arms from Russia, including twenty-eight Mi-35 and fifteen Mi-28NE attack helicopters. The first helicopters were delivered in 2013 and, along with the other military firepower on order, were on the front line within a couple of years in the battle to retake the city of Fallujah from IS.

Parting with those lucrative oil earnings isn't easy for Iraq, but in an ongoing conflict, buying weapons can be more import-ant than infrastructure or welfare spending. Russian arms have promised – and delivered – greater defence and security for Iraq and its people.

For Russia, that contract was a key contribution to an arms industry that's seen its export earnings increase five-fold since the turn of the millennium. It's part of a strategy to increase Russia's geopolitical powerbase – and its economic resilience. Russia is a heavyweight country with a lightweight economy; it's been strug-gling, and its old enemy the dollar has proved, so far, to be an unbeatable opponent. Twenty-first-century Russia is the big but feeble bear of the global economy, hamstrung by its history and left with an uneasy reliance on the dollar. If it is to get hold of dollars, it must give up its arms.

The end of the Cold War in 1991 is often seen as a triumph of lib-eralism. It certainly helped to reinforce the dollar's position. But the fall of communism was actually more about economic problems back home.

In 1955 the Warsaw Pact – a collective defence agreement for like-minded communist countries in the Eastern bloc – was signed. It set alarm bells ringing across the capitalist West and led to a massive build-up of arms – and a space race – on both sides. However, by the 1980s, the Soviet Union was running out of cash to pay for its weapons. Central planning had failed: the economy was running on empty, its people restless and unhappy, and the Soviet Union collapsed. It was the Cold War that shaped the arms industry as we know it today.

Iraq's dollar is just one of billions Russia now receives from defence-industry sales abroad. It is second only to the USA when it comes to selling weapons. And, like many commodities, guns tend to be priced in the international currency of trade: the dollar. The Cold War arms race wasn't just about conventional guns and grenades; the USSR was also investing heavily in nuclear arms, chemical weapons and nerve agents. At the end of that period, it was sitting on the world's largest stockpile of weapons. There was also a vast amount of know-how; Russia was at the cutting edge of research and development. It was time to cash in. Russia's companies were able to design, make and sell arms. They were owned either by the state or jointly by state companies and private investors such as Dmitry Sokolov. Until then, Russia had been manufacturing mainly to suit its own needs; now it was time to branch out.

It wasn't hard to spot potential customers. Even after the Cold War had thawed, Russia knew who its allies were: effectively those to whom America wasn't prepared to sell. The USA, with the largest arms industry on the planet, was supplying the rest of NATO and its allies in the Middle East, such as Saudi Arabia. Russia was able to target other newly emerging giants: China, India, some of the Middle East and much of South East Asia. Both buyers and sellers are wary of the other side; there's relatively little overlap in customer bases. Iraq is quite unusual in that its dollar could just have easily been spent on weapons from the USA instead – in fact, it is more likely to buy from the Americans. Iraq is one of the few that is 'friends' with both sides, but this means that Russia has to work extra hard to keep its custom.

Those taking on IS in Iraq with Russian arms were equally likely to have found themselves staring down the barrel of a gun with a 'made in Russia' or 'made in the USA' sticker. The human rights charity Amnesty International has traced this proliferation of weapons back to 'irresponsible' arms sales by both of the Cold War superpowers in the 1970s and 1980s. When Iran and Iraq went to war, the USSR was initially neutral – publicly anyway. But by the end of the conflict in 1988, Russia had become Iraq's biggest arms supplier. Three decades on, that meant IS extremists were 'like children in a sweetshop' according to Amnesty International. They were free to scoop up stockpiled weapons such as air-defence systems or Russian-made AK assault rifles. Many of those might have been sold via official streams but were subsequently poorly guarded, or fell into the wrong hands due to corruption and the chaotic regime change in Iraq.

IS fighters in Iraq probably couldn't believe their luck. Most other extremists – Boko Haram in Nigeria, for example, or Al-Qaeda – have to source their weaponry through illicit means. If the price is right, they can get what they want under the counter from unscrupulous vendors, selling small, portable weapons such as assault rifles, grenades, mortars and land mines, which are easy to smuggle undetected. By its nature, it's hard to put a price tag on the illicit small arms trade, but estimates put it at over $1 billion per year, aimed mostly at inflicting misery and terror on some of the world's most vulnerable people. One Russian gunrunner, Viktor Bout, a former military translator, became known as the 'merchant of death' after his role in illegal gunrunning in Congo and other countries in the 1990s. He was finally arrested in 2008 during an undercover sting, accused of trying to sell $15 million worth of weapons to the Revolutionary Armed Forces of Colombia (FARC), renowned for committing acts of terror. A court in New York sentenced him to twenty-five years in prison.

Even though it's the dark side of the global economy and can easily bleed into illegality, most arms sales are perfectly legal. In recent years, in a climate of increasing global tension and mounting military spending, Russia's arms sales have thrived and the country now has a quarter of the global market. It's a lucrative business, earning Russia around $15 billion a year from exports. Top sellers have included the S-300 long-range surface-to-air missile, the MiG 35 fighter jet, those helicopters bound for Iraq, and the T-90 super tank. It's not about having more weapons in your arsenal; it's about advancing military capability. While Russia was once wary of selling its most effective, up-to-date military gear abroad, it now relishes the opportunity. Such weapons can be enticing status symbols for newly prosperous economies; spending on military equipment by Vietnam, for example, tripled between 2012 and 2016 compared to the previous five years.

The arms race continues, and conflicts have become an opportunity for Russia to market – and test – its firepower. As tension has increased in the Middle East in the twenty-first century, spending on arms in the region has doubled, and Russia is taking an ever-larger slice of the pie. In 2015, Russia intervened in the Syrian civil war in support of President Assad. The war became, as one headline put it, a 'showroom for Russian arms sales', as Assad's troops demonstrated that firepower. The campaign cost Russia about $500 million, but it's estimated that it won about ten times as much in increased sales internationally. Dmitry Sokolov can't invest in conventional advertising – billboards and TV spots – but he doesn't need to. Wherever there's a successful arms manufacturer in the world, their national government will be pitching in with full marketing support.

It's not only about financial reward. National governments – including France and the UK – tend to wield companies like Dmitry's as weapons to achieve foreign policy objectives. Russia, for example, sees Syria as its key point of influence in the region. Its intervention in the civil war was labelled a 'game changer', but Russia was already the source of half the weapons sold to Syria, primarily because Russia had been looking to increase its allies in the Middle East in the wake of the Arab Spring. In addition, it was worried about the increased risk of Islamist extremism reaching its home soil.

However, it's a fickle game. Russia has indicated that it might switch its support if it looked as if the Assad regime would fall. The fast-paced shifts in geopolitical alliances mean there's always a risk that Dmitry's guns will eventually be trained on his motherland.

Internationally, eyebrows are soon raised if weapons are sold to regimes who use them to terrorise or indeed commit genocide against their own people. Russia's support of the Syrian regime, which stood accused of deploying chemical weapons, caused outrage in the West. But the Kremlin just accused those nations, including the USA and UK, of double standards, saying they were just as guilty of arming repressive regimes.

Most of the UK's arms exports, for example, went to Saudi Arabia in 2015, while in return the Saudis supplied the UK with oil. In violation of international humanitarian law, Saudi Arabia was enacting a bombardment of Yemen, costing thousands of lives. After the uprisings of the Arab Spring in North Africa, a report from the UK's own parliament concluded that successive governments had 'misjudged the risk that arms approved for export to certain authoritarian countries in North Africa and the Middle East might be used for internal repression'.

Foreign policy – and the thirst for export dollars – trumps human rights and international peace. The winners are companies such as Dmitry's and the countries they represent. Economic growth and the dollars a country earns might fluctuate from year to year, but the fortunes of arms traders are much more secure. The defence industry has its own protection against swings in the wider economic climate. Like food, arms can be considered an essential. Demand for military goods is somewhat 'inelastic', or near constant: spending to defend borders is one of the last things governments cut back on.

For Russia, the commercial aspect is enormous: in 2015, one in every twenty dollars of income from exports of goods came from selling arms. That doesn't mean, however, that its future military earnings are assured. Demand across the world is surging, but China is now taking on the established defence industry. A lack of investment and skilled scientists means that Russia is no longer at the cutting edge in weapons research and development.

Almost seventy per cent of the world's weaponry currently comes from the USA, France, UK and Russia: the traditional superpowers. But as the power of those countries is shifting, so too is their grip on the arms industry. In the not-too-distant future, Iraq may be sending its dollar to China instead. India so far remains a loyal customer but that too could change. Russia could find itself out in the cold in terms of both export earnings and power.

❧

Russia's attempt to integrate itself into the global economy – to assert the economic might it needs to match its political might – has not been easy. It needs those arms sales, because the rest of its economy is in trouble.

Across Russia's vast sprawling landscape, there's a wealth of natural resources, among them oil and gas. Russia can sympathise with Iraq over the paradox of plenty. Its oil and gas allow it to wield great power, for example deciding whether or not the lights stay on during those bitter winters in Western Europe. It could turn off the supply at the flick of a switch. But it's just as true that oil holds Russia in its grip, and the country, its competitors and the markets all know it.

Russia produces almost 11 million barrels of oil a day, second only to Saudi Arabia on average (and on occasion Russia has been known to supersede Saudi Arabia in this respect). The industry provides just over half of the Russian government's earnings and accounts for 70 per cent of Russia's export earnings. Russia is somewhat less dependent on those revenues than Saudi, but it's still enough to ensure oil is vital to Russia's stability. It's estimated that every $10 off the price of a barrel reduces Russia's GDP by almost 1.5 per cent. To balance its own books, Russia's government needs oil to be worth at least $100 per barrel. Moreover, it requires dollars to trade in oil, and that means its own currency suffers.

How has Russia, for all its size and military prowess, ended up in this position, so reliant on oil and on the currency of a perceived opponent? In the Soviet era, the central planning policies handed down from Moscow controlled what should be manufactured, and how much of it. The focus was less on making the machines and tools needed to keep industry functioning and more on weapons. Being closed off from the global economy led by the West meant there wasn't so much pressure to produce goods for export. There were relatively few enterprises, with power concentrated in a few hands, and they controlled many aspects of their workers' economic lives, providing everything from housing to furniture to food.

With little emphasis on producing the things people needed or wanted, there were shortages of basic products on shop shelves and the queues were notorious. Goods were snapped up when they were available and hoarded in bulk. A vast informal economy, worth up to a tenth of Russia's official economy, grew up to supply those who had the cash. The Cold War and the obsession with centralised planning doomed Russia to economic disadvantage.

In 1985, a new president, Mikhail Gorbachev, recognised that the system had faltered. His solution was *perestroika* and *glasnost* – restructuring and openness. He encouraged innovation and enterprise but his policies were piecemeal and insufficient to plug the gap in Russia's industry or, indeed, the gaps on shops' shelves. The kind of modern, large-scale manufacturing industry Russia needed was still not in sight.

Encouraged by the new outlook, banks in the West, particularly in Germany, gave the Soviet Union cautious backing through loans. Then a slump in the price of crude oil brought the energy-dependent economy of the Soviet Union to its knees. The lenders took fright and called in their loans. The bastion of communism found itself hobbled by capitalist markets, forced to sell gold to feed its population. Within a few years, the USSR was no more.

The mighty Soviet Union lay in fragmented tatters, but for those who had the ambition and muscle to pick through the ruins, there was treasure to be found. The end of the USSR heralded a ferocious but uneven outbreak of rapacious capitalism. The oligarchs – the Russian carpetbaggers – were those who had profited most from the new spirit of entrepreneurialism of the late 1980s and were now poised to make a killing. The cash-strapped government was selling off assets, in particular privatising its energy and financial industries, in deals that ended up benefiting powerful politicians and their cronies. They rapidly accumulated eye-watering wealth and with it a huge amount of influence over the economy and political system.

Among their number was Roman Abramovich, best known as the owner of Chelsea Football Club and exceptionally glitzy yachts and villas. Born to a humble family and orphaned at the age of two, he took advantage of the perestroika era by setting up a toy-production company while he was still a student. It gave him the springboard he needed. A skilled deal-maker, he later managed to acquire part of energy giant Sibneft. The rest is gold-plated history.

Vladimir Putin became president in 1999, vowing to take on the power of the oligarchs, and some messy battles ensued. His post-communist Russia might have been 'open' to the world, but Putin shared a common plight with his predecessors: his popularity, and Russians' incomes, continue to rise and fall in line with the price of a barrel of crude.

By 2006, the income taken home by the average Russian had doubled since the Soviet era, as oil income rose and taxes on some businesses were cut. Then the global financial crisis hit and, when the oil price fell in 2014, the cracks in Russia's economy were again exposed.

By 2015, the Russian economy was shrinking and investors were running scared. Prices in shops were soaring; Russians had to spend up to half their incomes on food alone. The *Moscow Times* gave an imaginative demonstration of how the population was struggling, reporting that the average Russian was now buying just two pairs of shoes per year, while his or her American counterpart was shelling out for almost eight. Lauren Miller was loading up, as women in Russia were cutting back, making do and mending.

In March 2014, Russia annexed Crimea and exercised military intervention in Ukraine, so the European Union, the USA and their allies decided to hit Russia in the pocket, imposing economic sanctions: restrictions on imports such as weapons or equipment for the oil industry; freezes on bank accounts and other Russian overseas assets; and travel bans for important individuals, to give just a few examples. The idea was to starve Russia of dollars. Russia imposed similar restrictions in return, including bans on some foodstuffs. Economic stalemate. It is estimated that the action might have cost Europe up to $100 billion but the cost to Russia, which was already facing recession, was even greater. For ordinary Russians the restrictions added to the pain of those lower oil prices. Bans on imported foods from the West sent prices up in Moscow. Growth slowed in response to what Putin called 'the unfriendly steps'. Yet, by 2017, Russia had failed to concede to a ceasefire.

Now we come to the crunch. Compounding all this was a drop in the value of Russia's currency. Concerns in the global currency markets – those great tides of speculation and sentiment – meant the rouble more than halved in value against the dollar. It was thought that Russia was too dependent on oil and was heading for trouble, so the speculators, herd-like, all started running away from its currency. The rouble crashed. In 2014, 30 roubles were needed to buy one dollar; at its nadir in early 2016 it was 85 roubles.

Why did that matter? It ramped up the price of imports, eating into Russians' spending power. To compound the general economic woes, the end of the Soviet era brought the end of subsidised farming, wreaking havoc on Russian agriculture. A large proportion of essentials such as milk, eggs and meat has to be shipped in by a wholesaler and paid for in the global currency of trade, dollars. This led to even greater demand for dollars, pushing down the value of the rouble yet further, and meaning sharply rising prices for Russian shoppers.

On top of that, large swathes of Russian debt were denominated in dollars. Servicing that became most costly. That wasn't such a big problem for the government, which had large foreign currency reserves, but it was a big headache for companies, which owed hundreds of billions of dollars overseas. In fact, governments and companies the world over risk facing a similar scenario if they have debts in dollars. A fall in the value of their currency against the dollar will affect their ability to repay – hitting profits, growth and even jobs. Given the ubiquity of borrowing in dollars on international markets, the UK's central bank concluded that a stronger dollar is, on the whole, bad news for global growth.

At the same time as the rouble was falling, the price of oil also dropped, which threatened export income. The silver lining of a weaker exchange rate was that it helped offset that drop, as oil is priced in dollars and Russia was now getting more roubles per dollar. But the benefits of a weaker rouble didn't go much further in helping the Russian economy. In another country, a weaker currency can make exports cheaper and therefore easier to sell abroad. People overseas then want more of the country's products, which in turn increases demand for the currency, which then gets stronger . . . In theory at least, it all balances out. The trouble is, apart from arms, Russia still doesn't *manufacture* much for export. And relying on oil to plug the gap is risky.

Russia was in a bind – a victim of the dollar's strength, and the rouble's weakness.

Historically, Russia's currency has been remarkably weak. Its name, which dates back to the thirteenth century, comes from the Russian word meaning 'to cut' or 'to hack'. That must have seemed pretty apt in the turbulent days of 2014 and, indeed, during the revolution of 1917, when its value dropped by almost one-third, causing huge price rises and fanning the revolutionary flames. Major historical events aside, one reason for the weakness of the rouble has been a lack of confidence. It's all in the mind.

Russia's rouble has one thing in common with the dollar: *they both have no intrinsic value.* All money is effectively a promise, be it a debt or a credit. Originally, the dollar was a promise to pay the bearer in gold. The dollar bill is an assurance of that promise; until 1934 each bill bore the words 'Will pay to bearer on demand . . .'. However, once the value of the dollar was no longer linked to gold, after the Bretton Woods agreement was terminated in 1971, it ceased to have a value of its own (it became what's known as a 'fiat' currency). Lauren Miller's dollar is a promise to her from the federal government; her deposit bank balance is effectively a promise made from the bank to her. And now, that dollar is a promise from the Iraqi government made in return for some weapons. However, these days, that promise is based on our shared belief in its value; not on something tangible.

The dollar's value, its might, is therefore based on trust: trust that it will be accepted as payment for goods and services worth one dollar; trust it will hold that value; and trust that the government can ensure that it will do so. The same goes for the rouble.

Money – currency – has three purposes. First, it has to be a generally accepted medium of financial exchange and repaying debt. It's all very well to exchange goats for wheat in a barter, but what if the goatherd doesn't need wheat and wants oil instead? The farmer must have a currency that the oil salesman will accept too. Second, it has to be a store of value: if you put aside one dollar on payday, it should still buy the same amount of wheat a week later (although inflation can eat into that a little). And, third, it's a unit of account, which means we can use it to measure the value of that goat. All 151 currencies of the world serve these purposes to varying degrees but it's the dollar, the currency of trade invoices, international debts and the safest type of reserves, that best fits the bill.

However, whether it's backed by gold or faith, if it isn't trusted, a currency can become useless.

In the former Soviet Union, a strange sort of parallel trading system emerged. The basics were often in short supply, and ordinary Russians faced mounting queues and prices to get hold of milk or eggs. By contrast, those with dollars to spend were ushered into well-stocked hard-currency stores. These lucky few were those who travelled or who had managed to forge business links abroad or who were dealing with foreign visitors. Tales were told of dollars being traded at a vastly inflated black-market rate by Moscow prostitutes who'd been engaged by foreign clients. As in much of the less-developed world, the plusher hotels in the big cities quoted rates in dollars. The greenback, a sign of financial stability and worth, was greatly coveted. Disillusioned by the Soviet

Union's ability to grow the economy and improve livelihoods, many ordinary Russians reluctantly came to view dollars as a route to a better life. Throughout the depths of the Cold War, Russia suffered the indignity of the dollar's powerful presence on its home soil.

In 2014, the rouble suffered a further crisis of confidence as Russian consumers and investors lost faith in the value of their currency and bought up televisions, jewellery and property. As money isn't just a means of buying what's needed or desired but is also a store of value, Russians were spending on big-ticket items they didn't need simply because they thought they'd retain their value better than the rouble in their pockets. Or they were snapping up safety-deposit boxes in banks, to stash away any foreign currency they'd managed to get hold of.

Adding to the pressure, Russian banks and oil companies were due to make payments worth tens of billions on their overseas debts, and needed to get their hands on dollars to do so. No one wanted roubles; everyone wanted dollars. Once confidence is gone, it can only get worse. It's a downward spiral.

The rouble had also crashed through the floor in 1998. Russia couldn't pay its debts, needed a bailout from the IMF and had to ramp up interest rates to an eye-watering 100 per cent. In other words, even the most straightforward loan would cost twice as much to pay back. In 2014, most could remember those times and few wanted to live through such hardship again.

Enter Elvira Nabiullina, head of Russia's central bank since 2013. The bespectacled daughter of a chauffeur and a factory worker has risen to become known as 'Putin's right-hand woman'. She put the boxing gloves on and went in for the fight, taking a number of risky measures to try to restore the rouble and with it Russia's confidence.

She put up interest rates, meaning that it was more profitable for Russian investors to hold money in rouble rather than dollar accounts. She limited the ability of commercial banks to speculate against the value of the rouble. Then she did something altogether radical: she more or less left the rouble to its own devices. For two decades previously, Russia had attempted to manage its currency in much the same way as China or Nigeria. The aim was to bring stability but it came at a cost. The central bank would plunder its valuable reserves in order to buy up roubles on the foreign exchange market while the currency's value was falling, thus pushing up demand and propping up its value. Ms Nabiullina said 'enough' and with a dose of tough love effectively set it free, leaving it to find its own value. The market reacted by punishing the rouble further over a period of several days.

It might have been seen as an ill-judged move but, at the start of 2015, the rouble actually began to stabilise. The central bank was able to use the reserves it would have put towards rescuing the currency to offer foreign-currency loans to commercial banks. That meant Russians could get dollars from their own banks; they didn't have to get them from elsewhere. The rouble was on the rise again. It was an unconventional approach, but Elvira Nabiullina appeared to have pulled off a neat trick. While her president's policy raised the hackles of Europe's politicians, its finance journals were lining up to acclaim her central banker of the year. Nabiullina had dealt a knockout blow but it was for this round alone. In the long-term fight, the dollar retains the upper hand.

Many countries use the dollar as a parallel currency, as the Soviet Union did, and as, to a degree, Russia still does. Even in 2017, over half the dollar notes in the world exist outside the USA, most likely in Latin American countries, or some former members of the Soviet Union.

Why is the dollar so popular in Latin America? One reason is trade. Ecuador and El Salvador don't actually have currencies of their own. In 2000, they officially 'dollarized', which means they adopted the American currency as their own, reasoning that it was simpler and more practical given the free-trade agreements they shared with the USA. They also viewed the stability of the dollar's value as likely to make their nations less prone to economic wobbles. Having a more trustworthy currency also can make a country a more attractive destination for foreign investment. In Panama, the dollar has been legal tender for over a century thanks to the Panama Canal. The construction of the canal led to a massive volume of international trade, so accepting the currency of that trade made practical sense for Panama.

Dollarizing officially – handing over some economic power to the USA – comes at a price. Being part of the dollar club means playing by its rules. Any country adopting the dollar as its official currency has to agree to be subject to American interest rates, which can have an impact on the exchange rate. US interest rates can be too low for another economy, thus encouraging too much borrowing, or too high, hitting consumers and businesses with crippling borrowing costs.

Countries can get around this by dollarizing 'unofficially', using the dollar as a parallel currency to its own. In most cases, this occurs when the official currency is in short supply or is suffering a crisis of confidence. This was the case in Argentina, where the peso was in freefall during an economic crisis at the start of this millennium and again in 2014. Many businesses – hotels and restaurants, for example – were quick to accept the dollar instead, guessing that it would hold its value better. From around 2010, those wishing to pay in dollars were frequently offered the 'blue' exchange rate, far more generous than the official one. In Argentina the use of a parallel currency brought into being a parallel economy. A division formed between those who could access dollars and those who couldn't. Prices were rising and the value of the peso was dropping – by 17 per cent in one two-day period in 2014. The only people who could protect the value of their savings and buy the goods they wanted at a reasonable price were those who could get their hands on dollars. In each episode, this created an insatiable demand for dollars that continued beyond the economic crisis itself and led to an environment ripe for corruption.

The dollar has been used as a parallel currency far from America's shores – in Cambodia, for example. Many people find trading in dollars is reassuring, in the same way that their governments head for the security of US government bonds. However, spending dollars can have disquieting implications. Wherever they're used in the world, they're accompanied by extraordinary legal powers for the USA.

These powers were made all too clear recently during the FIFA scandal. FIFA (Fédération Internationale de Football Association) is responsible for promoting and regulating the 'beautiful game' around the world. In 2015, the sporting world was rocked by a corruption and bribery scandal that reached FIFA's top tier when seven high-ranking officials were arrested in a dawn raid on a luxury Zurich hotel, the kind of operation usually reserved for terror suspects or gangland bosses in motels or 'safe houses' in seedy suburbs. More arrests followed; the men were accused of taking bribes that influenced the awarding of television rights and the location of prestigious tournaments. The investigation had been kick-started by the controversial decision to allocate the World Cup to Russia in 2018 and to Qatar in 2022. The sport's reputation was in shreds.

One of the most astonishing things was how this scandal came to light. Swiss police carried out the initial raids on Swiss soil but they were urged to do so by the Americans. The FBI had carried out an investigation that, it claimed, had uncovered racketeering and fraud spanning twenty-four years, and it brought criminal charges against several FIFA executives. The US attorney general, Loretta Lynch, accused them of 'corruption that is rampant, systemic and deep-rooted'.

Why did the USA care so much? After all, soccer, as it's known there, is still somewhat a novelty, with viewing figures lagging far behind those for American football, basketball and baseball. But it matters because the kickbacks were made in dollars and the USA doesn't like its greenbacks getting dirty. It has legal authority over any transaction that 'touches' the USA – that is if it involves dollars that have at some point gone through American banks or 'touched' its financial system. Stringent money-laundering laws mean that banks and their employees have to keep meticulous records of where money has come from and where it goes.

The long arm of American law truly is long and national boundaries are no barrier. It's not afraid to flex its muscles the world over: not least where the dollar is in constant use, in Latin America. Brazil-based Odebrecht is the region's largest construction conglomerate. It's virtually unknown in the USA but it holds the questionable distinction of having signed the world's largest 'leniency deal', worth $2.6 billion, with the authorities in the USA, Brazil and Switzerland, after confessing to widespread corruption

– specifically paying large bribes in return for contracts across Latin America.

It's not just dodgy dealings. The US has equal jurisdiction over any transaction anywhere that has involved its financial system – paying for a hotel or food in hard currency in Moscow, for example. The Americans are, in effect, empowered by the dollar to act as the world's police. America's wide-ranging powers aren't just financial; it can also, for example, prosecute over emails that have been carried by an American internet server, something that internet giants such as Microsoft and Google have challenged.

Many countries resent it – not least Russia. Why does America have the authority to discredit the decision to hold the World Cup in Moscow? Russia itself surely wouldn't acquiesce to an American extradition request, but, in this case, it doesn't really matter. PR is everything in sport and business. Brands such as Sony and Emirates Airlines, so keen to have their logos plastered over previous World Cups, have steered clear of this one. The scandal has turned the FIFA brand toxic. It's the most emphatic evidence yet of the dollar's insidious influence. For this and other reasons, Russia has banded together with some unlikely teammates to tackle the dollar's supremacy.

The US currency's position at the top of the tree was cemented at that summit in Bretton Woods in 1944. At that same meeting, the IMF and the World Bank were created. They were tasked with ensuring financial stability, reducing poverty and encouraging economic growth. Critics say they are also about maintaining the dollar's position by ensuring it remains the core 'reserve currency'. That means it's not only the main currency for trade but is also the medium in which countries store their cash, those foreign reserves held by the central bank. That keeps the dollar in demand, ensuring its strength, and giving the USA undue influence. Over the years, the dollar has been joined by its top-tier stablemates, the euro, the pound sterling and the yen, all deemed relatively safe ways of holding cash because of their sturdy originating economies. Around 85 per cent of funds held in foreign reserves is in one of those four currencies. America, the Eurozone, the UK and Japan don't, however, represent 85 per cent of global economic activity, population or land mass.

So why not attempt to break the big boys' stranglehold? In July 2014, a summit in Fortaleza, Brazil, was led by what's become known as the BRIC countries: Brazil, Russia, India and China, identified at the start of the century as the next big things. Between them, they account for nearly a quarter of the world's economic activity. Russia has the smallest population of the four, but Russians individually are typically wealthier than inhabitants of the rest of the BRIC community, giving Russia the edge.

The BRIC foreign ministers were shown in the official photos holding hands, but the summit was more than a love-in of second-tier countries. Among myriad trade deals, they set up their own rival to the World Bank, the New Development Bank, and created a joint cash reserve fund. They set out plans to create their own reserve currency. China led the charge. If the yuan were to become a reserve currency, it would be more stable, and China would have to hold fewer reserves of other currencies. Although China would be the main winner, by banding together the BRICs saw a way to challenge the dominance of the West, even if it might carry some political risk.

Overall, though, the BRIC countries' attempt stalled. It's partly because they've failed to achieve the stellar growth this century that many had anticipated. China's currency has gained more credibility, and some would say that the dollar's supremacy is under threat. However, the yuan remains some way off being regarded as in the same league. China and Russia did try to bypass the dollar by agreeing to a direct currency swap, using the rouble and the yuan to pay for goods bought from each other instead. However, in the event China has used far fewer roubles than was hoped: the oil it bought from Russia was much cheaper in 2014 and the lower cost was not compensated for by an increase in demand.

The paradox of plenty, the curse of black oil, was attacking Russia from all sides. To insulate against its effects, Russia needs to diversify and grow its exports. And if it can become more self-sufficient through diversification, it's less reliant on imports, less vulnerable to swings in the rouble and so less susceptible to the dollar's power.

Selling arms might seem a questionable move, fuelling destruction around the globe. But to Russia and other arms-exporting countries, in the cold logic of economic accountancy, it's a lucrative earning stream. Russia does have other options: oil apart, it's blessed with natural resources ranging from diamonds to iron. Actually, it earned more from exporting foodstuffs such as grains in 2015 than it did from selling military helicopters and the like. Grain prices, like oil prices, can be unpredictable, varying wildly. Selling arms would be a more reliable business – if Russia can get it right. It would be an important step in diversification away from oil. It's a growing area of business it will have to work to hang on to, for the sake of Dmitry Sokolov and the Russian population as a whole.

The average worker in Russia earns $300 a month; in a good month, men such as Dmitry can earn a thousand times as much. It's an even more extreme disparity than is found in the West. Foreign homes, yachts and even footballs clubs are within the reach of these oligarchs. Yet, for all his riches, Dmitry treats each dollar with care. Who knows how long the good times will last before the Chinese catch up? He may look for a bank to lodge it with but Russia's banks are seen as relatively unsophisticated and operate under inconsistent and restrictive rules. More important, they're seen as risky, although no one's quite sure how risky. The opaque way in which Russia's banks are managed and supervised by the state makes them hard to inspect, and this makes potential customers nervous – particularly Dmitry, with his millions to deposit.

Russian banks are even more unpopular following the sanctions and restrictions imposed by the USA and the EU. Some Russian banks aren't allowed to dabble in the international markets, buying bonds or shares there, for example, or raising loans, which has hampered their ability to make loans to businesses at home. Energy companies were prevented from importing the sophisticated machinery needed to locate and extract oil. Following the shooting down of flight MH17 in Ukraine, the maker of Buk missiles, the state-owned Almaz–Antey defence giant, was put on the restricted list. Almaz–Antey missiles, along with the arms made by another twelve Russian companies, were banned from sale in the EU or the USA. The West refused to continue to share technology that might be used to construct defence systems. Several of Dmitry Sokolov's cronies and rivals found their foreign bank accounts and assets were seized and frozen.

Against this backdrop, where is Dmitry to keep his dollar? When Cyprus started to offer citizenships in return for investment, it became a popular destination for Russian money. Those passports promised a life of sun in Limassol, and they could also allow Russians somewhere to hide ill-gotten gains – or 'launder' money. Not every dollar acquired in Russia – or anywhere else – is above board. Keen to escape the scrutiny and demands of their own government, by 2017 more than a thousand rich Russians had taken Cypriot passports.

Managing the new Russian wealth has been big business for banks across Europe, but if it is not handled properly the consequences can be severe. Just ask Deutsche Bank, Germany's biggest bank. Its Moscow branch was set up in 1998, when international banks were elbowing each other aside to get a slice of the post-glasnost gold rush. They saw an easy way to make money in a previously underdeveloped but rapidly booming post-Soviet economy.

In 2017, Deutsche had to pay record fines to the American and British financial watchdogs when it was found guilty of aiding and abetting money laundering, a process by which 'dirty' money acquired through illegal means – for example, extortion, bribery, or arms smuggling – is disguised, 'washed clean', so that it looks as if it was earned legally.

Deutsche set up a system, known as 'mirror trading', whereby wealthy Russians could swap their roubles for another currency. An order would be placed on behalf of a customer to buy Russian shares using roubles, typically a few million dollars' worth. At the same time, another order was placed to sell the same amount of the shares elsewhere in return for dollars or pounds. The second order would be placed on behalf of a different offshore company. The proceeds fetched up in the most unlikely of places: paying the school fees of oligarchs' children in London, for example.

Over two and a half years Deutsche Bank carried out more than 2,000 of these trades, involving billions of dollars. Newspapers including the *Guardian* have called such activities 'Russia's biggest business', dodgy deals becoming commonplace in the scramble for wealth and power after the break-up of the Soviet Union. Mirror trades even have their own Russian nickname: *konvert*.

Bankers and their institutions face hefty penalties – including possibly a prison sentence – if they don't clamp down on money laundering. However, in this case, a blind eye appears to have been turned. As dollars were involved in these sordid deals, they incurred the full wrath of the American authorities. Once again, the USA was permitted to act as a financial policeman far beyond its own borders. Deutsche Bank faced damaging headlines. In Germany, leading magazine *Der Spiegel* claimed the 'proud institution became a self-serve buffet for a few, who became fantastically rich', accusing the bank of 'egoism . . . incompetence, mendacity . . . decadence, arrogance'. The lengthy article, which detailed several other scandals the institution had been embroiled in, including mis-selling and mismanagement, was titled 'How a Pillar of German Banking Lost Its Way'. In 2017, Deutsche cut back the scale of its operations in Moscow.

Germany itself remains a magnet for wealthy Russians. The richest country in Europe was also the most reluctant to give sanctions its blessing, perhaps because 40 per cent of the gas used by its 82 million people comes from Russia. If Germany pushes too far, it fears Russia could shut down the gas pipeline and leave its residents in the cold. It is notable that Russia's gas industry has escaped sanctions, and Germany has angrily opposed any widening of sanctions that could impact that industry. In this uncertain climate, Russia still feels it has some sway over Germany.

Those German bank accounts are now facing tougher rules and more scrutiny. Maybe they will become less attractive. But Dmitry still wants to park his dollar somewhere safe, with a good return. He's still looking to Germany, and what, literally, could be safer than houses?

7

The trials of a blended family

Russia to Germany

The brochure for the cream-coloured Mitzi apartment block, with its chrome fittings, oak flooring and manicured lawns, hints at an enviable urban lifestyle: 'TRENDY, EXCITING, CEN-TRAL LIVING'. It's an expansive description of a compact space. These are in fact micro-apartments with a floor area of between 24 and 48 square metres. Squeezing in even a small family would be a struggle, but that doesn't bother Dmitry Sokolov, as he has no intention of moving there.

This is Berlin, one of the most vibrant and cosmopolitan cities in the world. It's a magnet that draws people from the rest of Germany, the rest of Europe and from countries further afield. Like many European cities, it is also a magnet for investment – from Russia and elsewhere. Investors from Singapore, China and even Israel will be eyeing those apartments. They represent a new breed of wealthy investor and they are changing the global property map. Dmitry's dollars are, even in a small way, helping to build Berlin. In order to buy his little piece of prosperity, he exchanges his dollars for euros with Germany's biggest bank, Deutsche Bank. The dollar must take a back seat – temporarily – as we enter Euroland and explore another great economic story of our age.

Money has been pouring into cities across Europe in recent years, and not just in the Eurozone. Londoners lucky enough to be able to afford a flat in one of the new city-centre blocks are likely to be competing with buyers from around the globe. Houses, apartments, office blocks and land in the British capital are estimated to have attracted over $150 billion of foreign money between 2009 and 2016. Investors need to ensure they're buying in a place that has a friendly approach to foreign investment. Unlike Canada or Switzerland, London doesn't place heavy restrictions or penalties on foreign ownership. But as its popularity has increased, so too have prices and competition. That has made Berlin an increasingly attractive option.

Berlin is the biggest residential buy-to-let market in Europe. The popularity of renting there has led to one of the world's lowest home-ownership rates. About half of Germans own their homes – far fewer than in Spain, for example – and the home-ownership rate in Berlin is less than half the national average. Some 40,000 people move to Berlin every year and, as the demand for good-quality housing is rising faster than it can be met, they can expect to pay a hefty premium. The property market here, in one of the world's most vibrant and popular cities, is an attractive one, and the internet has opened it up to international investors who are looking to park their dollars somewhere safe, offering a good return.

Why are these European cities so relaxed about letting in the world's landlords? Some argue that this foreign investment stimulates construction, in particular house building, helping to satisfy the growing demand for homes from a rising population. Large-scale investors might also be willing to back the most show-stopping and prestigious buildings: London's towering Shard, for example, was funded by Qatari money. The rich might also invest more widely in a country, or bring their entrepreneurial skills with them. In short, they can increase a country's wealth.

As with all foreign investment, there are upsides as well as downsides. Some feel the new owners might not prioritise the needs of the local population. In Berlin, there was outrage when an apartment building was earmarked for sale to an investment company from Luxembourg that was intending to sell it on. The outcry was understandable. Rents had soared by 50 per cent over a decade, kick-started by the sale of over a hundred thousand council flats into private and often foreign hands between 2002 and 2007. This building was taken into public ownership, after a local government successfully exercised its right of purchase.

London's mayor, Sadiq Khan, has criticised foreign investors for using the city's homes simply as 'gold bricks for investment'. It's a feeling shared by some residents. Foreign owners renting out their properties extract cash from the country, but the impact is even worse when they leave those properties empty, either for their own use or for resale. Such investors have been labelled 'buy-to-leavers'. There is concern that all this foreign competition might simply be pushing house prices out of the reach of locals. Across London, one study found foreign buyers purchasing 7 per cent of available properties. They were concentrated mainly in the wealthiest enclaves of the city, making up almost half of those buying properties with a price tag of over £1 million in central London. Does it matter to the wider population? It does if the consequence is that they're being forced out to the suburbs or beyond.

The prevalence of ownership from abroad, tapping into another country's wealth and income, seems set to thrive as new millionaires are created around the world. There is an abundance of money on the move. Just as large-scale investors and governments look to make the most of their money with FDI (foreign direct investment), so individuals are increasingly investing overseas both for financial gain and for prestige. However, as prices rise in Berlin, investors will start turning to new, cheaper locations, such as up-and-coming cities like Warsaw. Globalisation means nothing stands still for long.

With its booming cities, and for many other reasons, Germany is a magnet for all kinds of investment and is likely to remain so for the foreseeable future. It's the powerhouse economy at the heart of Europe, famous for the strength of its manufacturing and for selling its products all over the world.

Deutsche Bank might have run into trouble with its dealings with Russia, but Dmitry Sokolov's dollars have now entered one of the most stable – indeed, in some eyes, boring – banking systems in the world. Germany's big banks, such as Deutsche, have been interlinked with the rollercoaster fortunes of Europe's richest economy for 150 years. Deutsche was founded in 1870 and in its early years it played a leading role in creating some of the German industrial giants still thriving today: pharmaceuticals company Bayer, for example, or motor specialist Daimler-Benz.

In the quest for growth and prosperity, Germany had followed the steps of Walter Rostow's development plan closely, unlike India (see Chapter 4), and relatively early on. By the time of the First World War, Germany was already hugely developed, with a lot of industrial capacity, including the production of armaments. Finance, industry and military armaments have always been linked, as the money and know-how required for arms development benefit industrial development, and vice versa. The machine age heralded a new era of mechanised warfare.

The First World War changed Germany's fortunes. Reeling physically and financially from defeat, its government had to pay $33 billion (or $450 billion in today's money) to other countries for civilian damage and reparation costs. It needed to take out some big foreign loans, and the biggest came from America, in dollars. Germany had been printing money during the war to pay for its military operations. After hostilities ceased, the wounded country struggled to produce the goods its citizens desperately needed. There was too much money chasing few goods. Germany's currency, the mark, rapidly lost value as prices soared. Legendary tales are told of workers having to collect wages in wheelbarrows, or of a loaf of bread costing millions of marks. The exchange rate plummeted as confidence in Germany evaporated. In 1914 the exchange rate was 4.2 German marks to the dollar; within a decade it was 4.2 trillion marks.

In 1924 stability was finally restored through a combination of a coalition government, a new bank, the Reichsbank, and a new currency, the Reichsmark. The old money was burned. Then, in 1929, just as Germany was starting to enjoy better times, came the Wall Street Crash. American banks were quick to call in their loans. German banks didn't have enough dollars (or rather the currency to buy them); some smaller institutions even collapsed. The economy slumped and unemployment rose dramatically, leading to protest and unrest. Against this backdrop of disillusionment, National Socialism – the Nazis – gained ground.

During the Nazi era, Deutsche Bank played an active part in financing Hitler's regime, including the expropriation of Jewish businesses. It was a dark period that the bank has addressed with honesty. After the Second World War, with the country having lost the majority of its housing and a third of its farming capacity, Deutsche threw itself into ensuring West Germany had access to funds for its so-called 'economic miracle'. By this point, the defeated nation had been split into zones, variously controlled by Western and Soviet superpowers. This geographic and eventually political division led to the country splitting into West and East Germany, and the erection of the Berlin Wall.

It can be argued that one lesson of Germany's economic collapse is that with the global power of the dollar comes responsibility: responsibility for economic and financial stability. So the United States initiated the multi-billion dollar Marshall Plan to rebuild the democracies of Western Europe. FDI, 1940s-style. Already in possession of the foundations of an industrialised economy, West Germany looked like a guaranteed success, a sure bet. And, of course, it provided the USA with a sturdy ally against communism.

Those foreign dollars helped West Germany to regain its position as the most potent state in Europe, becoming the leader in twentieth-century industrial excellence and in banking, as well as being Europe's most powerful economy. After the Second World War, arms production across Germany was initially banned but the country could make the most of its previous strength and expertise. It channelled its efforts into a stable manufacturing economy, backed by strong banks and long-term investment strategies, and fuelled by worldwide exports.

The German 'economic miracle' was echoed in Japan – also the site of a massive rebuilding effort in the post-war period. Backed by cash and goodwill, both were able to make a fresh, emphatic start in a rapidly industrialising world. They focused on manufacturing and increasing the standard of living across their populations. They were beacons of the modern industrial economy, their brands household names and bywords for quality, efficiency and the latest technology. (For those who'd suffered under Japanese or German military might during the war, it was a bewildering, occasionally even offensive, state of affairs.) The roots of German and Japanese resurgence lay in the confluence of money and machines, and those who'd backed their rehabilitation found themselves floundering, economically, in their wake. The victors weren't getting all the spoils.

The formula paid off decisively for Germany and Japan. By the 1990s, the standard of living in both countries was among the best in the world, and their economies were outranked only by the USA. Fifty years after the two countries' crushing military defeat, German and Japanese products were everywhere, pulling in pounds, dollars and yen from across the globe.

Germany's post-war experience offers a sharp contrast to that of some of its European neighbours. Greece, for example, also benefited from a large cash injection to jump-start its industrial sector after the Second World War, and it saw some miraculous growth. However, it wasn't to last. There were two key differences between Greece and its northern counterpart. First, Greece didn't emerge from a painful civil war until 1950, and only then did the economic clean-up operation start. Second, it was starting from a much lower base. After the war, the average Greek had an income less than half that of the average German. Its banking sector and its industrial base were far less sophisticated.

The money, when it arrived, really did spark Greece into life. As its manufacturing sector boomed, it enjoyed some of the fastest growth rates in Europe during the 1950s and 1960s. It was catching up, until it was hit hard by the soaring oil price in the early 1970s. Many countries suffered, but in Greece the rise in fuel costs coincided with the collapse of the military dictatorship. The economy was left in a state of paralysis and ordinary Greeks' incomes failed to grow at all between 1979 and 1987. Their country was falling behind again, with manufacturing industry struggling to compete and banks less flush with cash.

The Greek government decided to tackle the situation by spending more cash. It created vast swathes of jobs in its already bloated public sector. To pay for this strategy, it had to borrow on the money markets, but the wariness of investors meant that interest rates were high and it cost the Greeks more to borrow. The loss of confidence dragged down the value of the Greek currency, the drachma.

Then, in the 1990s, its neighbours offered a life raft, one that meant the fortunes of Germany and Greece becoming inextricably linked. It was the culmination of a journey of increasing integration, trade and prosperity across Europe, which had all started with the end of the Second World War and the influx of dollars prompted by the Marshall Plan.

cco

After the war a like-minded group of nations – Belgium, France, West Germany, Italy, Luxembourg and the Netherlands – came together politically and economically to form a 'family' unit, under the unwieldy banner of the European Coal and Steel Community. Their aim was to secure lasting peace through closer bonds, and through a shared interest: trade. As their bonds grew, they soon agreed to stop charging each other to trade, and controlled food production jointly. This communal and collaborative approach led them to adopt the label of the European Economic Community (EEC) or Common Market.

The EEC family welcomed some new arrivals in the early 1970s – the UK, Denmark and Ireland. In the wake of the oil-price spike, it altered its rules so that richer countries could help out poorer members. The tribe was enlarged yet again with Portugal, Spain and Greece joining in 1980s. In 1993, the EEC changed its name to the European Union.

The biggest shake-up came when the Berlin Wall fell in 1990 and, almost overnight, some of the wider European clan came out of the cold and wanted in. It took some time, but by 2007 eleven new members had joined from the old Eastern bloc, the so-called accession countries. In the meantime, Sweden, Austria and Finland had also joined. By 2013, the initial family of six had become twenty-eight. By 2016, over 500 million people were living within the borders of the European Union.

Like all blended families, this group was incredibly diverse. The make-up, fortunes, needs and experiences of its members varied dramatically. The economy of founding father Germany, for example, is 150 times the size of new arrival Estonia's, and consequently the country was able to exercise the political power that came with being one of the biggest in the group. At the heart of the EU has always been the French–German relationship, a close kinship between Europe's two richest economies. So why were the newer, smaller members so keen to join? What was in it for them?

The EU wanted to create a trading bloc, a market for buying and selling products to rival the USA's, and to counter competition from developing countries. With a view to peaceful and easy living, the

Single European Act was signed in 1986 to allow free trade across borders with the movement of people, money, services and goods: the 'four freedoms'.

Free movement of goods means items can be sold from one European country to another without tariffs being added to the purchase price. Imported goods don't have to face lengthy customs checks at the borders, and the same rules and regulations apply across the whole area. EU countries also present a united front to outsiders – a customs union – so whichever EU country China, for example, is selling to, it'll face the same sort of tariffs or checks. Chinese manufacturers might undercut their European competitors due to lower wages, but EU barriers slow down goods arriving from China and might give European manufacturers a competitive edge when it comes to selling to the rest of Europe. The same is true of smaller EU nations, and that benefit could be even more crucial for them: up to 80 per cent of Hungary's trade, for example, is with the rest of the EU.

These rules have now been in force for a quarter of a century. They were designed to make European goods cheaper, and open up more markets for their manufacturers. It's hard to know how much the creation of a European single market has helped, but statistics offer some guidance. The OECD estimates that trade between EU countries is over 70 per cent higher than it would have been without the single market. This is important for European businesses and it also enables Europe to preserve its role in the booming global marketplace. The World Trade Organization claims world trade rose ninefold between 1980 and 2011, and by the end of that period developing countries accounted for half of those exports. In other words, the EU would have been a far less productive and prosperous area without the single market. Its member states would have been less able to hold their own against cheaper competitors.

The single market seemed to be working so well that the EU decided to go one step further and develop its own currency: the euro. In 1992, twelve members of the EU signed up for the further integration that the euro symbolised. The idea was to create a core currency for trade and bank reserves to rival the dollar, and to replace members' domestic currency.

Prior to the euro's introduction it was estimated that if a tourist travelled through all the EU countries, changing $1 into the local currency as he went, he'd have lost almost 50 cents to commission by the end of his journey. A single currency would enable individuals and businesses to compare prices in different areas. This should make it easier for companies to plan their spending on items from abroad and, given increased certainty, they would be more likely to invest and create jobs. Having a unified currency was intended to facilitate trade.

The Eurozone, as it has become known, would be seen as a more successful, stable bet for investment, able to attract even more dollars from the likes of Dmitry Sokolov. Smaller, poorer countries would get the kudos and trading links that come from being part of a major team. Greece, for example, would lose its national currency, but it would gain one that would signify greater credibility and stability, benefiting from the more robust economic credentials of Germany and France. Germany would be giving up the currency that had propelled it to post-war prosperity but, in return, it would become the powerful leader of a growing pack. Hell-bent on maintaining its international exports, it would even find them being boosted. Sharing a currency with weaker neighbours would mean that currency being likely to be weaker than if

Germany were to go it alone, but as a result Germany's exports would become cheaper and more attractive when it came to trying to sell to Asia or the USA.

It sounds like a great plan. But switching currencies isn't simple; it's not one-size-fits-all. To prepare for the big move, Eurozone countries had to get into shape. They needed to meet the conditions set out in a rulebook called the Maastricht Treaty to ensure their economies were aligned, or converging, which would allow for stability.

As is obvious from looking at just the two examples of Germany and Greece, the individual economies of Europe are vastly different. The headline economic figures don't give the full story of the rich histories, the diverse peoples and the localised industries that have developed over hundreds of years.

According to the rules, Eurozone governments were meant to be borrowing less than 3 per cent of their GDP per year. This figure represented the gap between their spending and tax earnings, and was meant to demonstrate they were solvent and stable. Individual governments still had control over their own taxes and spending, but their degree of freedom was constrained by this requirement to – broadly – balance the books. When a government borrows, that adds to the stock of public debt it might have accumulated over many, even hundreds, of years. Again, for solvency's sake, the Eurozone members were meant to have debt roughly in line with each other, at no more than 60 per cent of their GDP.

They also had to demonstrate that their interest rates and their inflation rates were similar. Interest rates are the primary tool used to control spending and saving in an economy, and consequently they affect growth and inflation. Having similar interest and inflation rates would signify that their economies were pulling in the same direction, converging and at a similar stage in their cycles. This was important because in future, interest rates for all members of the Eurozone would be set at one level by the European Central Bank (ECB) to control growth and inflation. A single currency necessitates a single interest rate.

In practice, the rules were blurred somewhat: bent and interpreted creatively for both big guns such as Germany and wayward upstarts such as Greece. Many critics of the euro experiment at the time thought this was outrageous. But the political leaders and economic architects of that experiment were inclined to gloss over all that and fudge the figures to get their plans under way. Some of the tiny flaws that crept through just might have widened into gaping wounds a decade down the line.

The UK was among the initial cynics. Its government set up its own tests for joining the euro, looking at the impact on prices, jobs (in financial services, for example), whether its economy was actually aligned with Europe, and what might happen if an economic crisis hit. Ultimately, it was asking whether that one 'uniform' designed by the EU – the euro and the single interest rate that went with it – could fit all family members without bursting at the seams at the first sign of strain. The checklist became a study that filled nineteen volumes, analysing everything from which countries the UK traded with to the price of chocolate bars around the continent. While the differing price of a Mars Bar didn't seal the deal on its own, the UK concluded that its economy wasn't sufficiently converged with the rest of the Eurozone. In fact, in concluded it was more aligned with its old colonial cousin, the USA. It said a polite 'No, thank you', and kept hold of the pound.

After a bit of creative accounting, the euro first appeared in 1999, and the national currencies of its twelve founder members were replaced by euro notes and coins in 2002. By 2016, the euro was the national currency of nineteen countries, with all their differences of size and fortune. Their combined GDP rivals China's (although, with a far smaller population in the Eurozone, income per person is much higher). It is, however, the currency of more than 340 million people – a population larger than America's.

The USA's central bankers had initially feared that the euro could topple the dollar from pole position as the key global currency. But the cracks soon started to show. Countries whose currencies had previously been judged on their own merits – with the good or bad fortune that entailed – were now subject to the force of this powerful new currency, which was competing against the dollar, yen, yuan and pound sterling. Its fortunes didn't have much to do with the economic reality in each country; rather, it reflected the average European climate.

Despite their shared philosophy, these countries really were all different, and didn't speak with one voice. Italy, Germany and France alone make up over half of the Eurozone's GDP. When it comes to setting interest rates, their needs dominate – and it is interest rates that have caused many of the problems.

Central banks usually set interest rates with the aim of fine-tuning the economy. At the beginning of the euro experiment, the ECB set interest rates in order to help the largest economy, Germany, which needed a boost, as it was suffering higher unemployment. A rate cut lowered German borrowing costs, put more money in the average German's pocket, and made Germans more inclined to spend than to save. However, the rates were too low for the Irish economy, which needed to cool down. A rate cut there encouraged people to take on more credit and spend more. Borrowing in Ireland was growing at the fastest rate in the

Eurozone, and fuelled a growth spurt. The country was nicknamed the Celtic Tiger. High streets were awash with cash; retailers felt confident about putting up prices faster. Inflation rose. Mortgages were more affordable. A property boom ensued in Dublin. Boom tends to be followed by bust, as demand runs out of steam; Ireland ran true to form. Fifteen years on, unemployment in Ireland was higher than when it had joined the Eurozone.

Ireland in particular had teething problems with its Eurozone membership, but, until the 2008 crisis, most of the other economies had been bumbling along fine, with just the occasional hiccup. The clan's wild child, Greece, had higher levels of public debt than the rest. It had been living way beyond its taxpayers' means. Investors who had lent Greece money were able to indulge the overspending as long as the good times continued. If the good times *had* continued, perhaps the Eurozone economies would have drifted towards a path of closer integration, better equipped for stormy weather in the future. Instead, when the lean times struck in 2008, the group's vulnerabilities and the full extent of its members' differences were exposed.

As we'll see in Chapter 8, American banks ultimately put an end to those good times. European and US banks took a hit from loans that weren't going to be paid back in America. Lending dried up; jobs and growth were hit. Governments found their borrowing increasing rapidly as the tax take fell and they had to pay out more in welfare. Suddenly, Greek and Italian public debt looked alarmingly high, their banks in trouble. And growth prospects for the two countries were bleak.

The rate of interest a government pays on its bonds (that is, when it borrows) reflects perceptions of that government's solvency, wealth and credibility. That the interest rates on government bonds differed so much across the Eurozone was another sign of how the individual economies weren't converging, regardless of sharing a single currency. Investors tried to offload their Greek bonds, scared that the government might go bust. Greeks had to pay more if they wanted to borrow.

By contrast, because the base interest rate within each country is set by the ECB for the whole Eurozone, the worst-hit countries didn't have the freedom to cut their own rates, which might have encouraged their people to spend more, and thereby boost their struggling economies. The economies most affected – Portugal, Italy, Greece and Spain (which were slapped with the unfortunate acronym 'PIGS') – made up just one-fifth of the Eurozone's economy, and so were not in a position to dictate the rate for the rest of its members.

They might have sought support from its fellow members at this point, but Germany made it clear it wasn't the responsibility of its taxpayers to bail out its struggling Eurozone relatives. Linked only by a common currency, the ailing members were effectively left to their woes.

Fresh from one crisis, the guardians of global finance were wary of another one. So the IMF and the EU waived some of Greece's debts and handed it some emergency cash. As with parents rescuing a recalcitrant teenager, the bailout came with strings attached. Greece was told it had to reduce its spending and get its house in order. Austerity measures included big cuts to pensions and public jobs, and hikes in tax. Already on the breadline, Greeks were outraged. Why shouldn't Germany and its other richer neighbours foot more of the bill, be a bit more charitable and understanding? Why should hanging out in the big boys' club mean playing by their tough rules? Greece objected to what it perceived as Germany being heavy-handed. Moreover, it was bristling that its richer counterpart may have been unfairly favoured by EU policy. Rebelling against the cost-cutting its creditors were insisting on, Greece elected an anti-austerity government. The haggling over the cuts and hand-outs continued.

Five years on, Greek pensions have been cut a dozen times, resulting in a 40 per cent drop in value. Families have borne the hardship. The economy remains wobbly and investors nervous. The question of whether Greece would be better off shipping out and leaving the Eurozone hangs in the air. It would mean reasserting control over its own interest rates, and therefore having more control over its own fortunes. On the other hand, Greece would lose the 'credibility' of belonging to the Eurozone and have to face the massive adjustment of transferring back to its own currency. The switch might possibly prompt a crisis of confidence in the Greek economy, and in the economy of the Eurozone as a whole.

Meanwhile, a few hundred miles north, its richer Eurozone siblings are springing back to life. The *Financial Times* was quick to hail the Eurozone as the 'surprise economic story of 2017'. Growth in the area has, since 2015, outpaced that in the USA. Even the PIGS were doing their bit, expanding at a healthy clip. At one point in late 2017, the Greek economy was growing faster than the UK's. But the overall numbers mask the underlying situation. Greece is grappling with its own problems. The stability of Italian banks continues to trouble investors. Whatever the Eurozone might look like on the surface, this is not Happy Families. The economies haven't converged. A comparison of prices in New York and rural Virginia, for example, will demonstrate that the cost of living will always differ from place to place owing to variations in demand and supply. However, in the Eurozone, the variation in the price of a Mars Bar can indicate that the economies are growing at different rates, experiencing different fortunes, and reacting to shocks in different ways.

On a global scale, the fledgling euro had faltered. It hadn't quite become the rival to the dollar that had initially been expected. There were fundamental differences in what these two single currencies represented. Both the dollar and the euro unite a large geographical area with very diverse populations, although the USA does have a common language. Both have their interest rates controlled and money issued by a single central bank; that is, they have monetary union. They both have a single market, with goods, people and money able (with a few exceptions) to roam freely across the area. In the USA, the bulk of tax money is collected and spent centrally, by the federal union, but in the Eurozone, each country is responsible for its own taxes and government spending, controlling its own finances, and there's no pooling of resources (give or take a few small areas). Each Eurozone member picks its own government, which is free to decide how to spend its own budget and, largely, how to run its own country. There's no fiscal union – and there's no political union. If America is doing well as a whole, a struggling individual state can be helped by centralised taxation and distribution of wealth. But that doesn't happen in the Eurozone, even though member states don't have complete control over their own finances.

This has led some to argue that even more central integration is needed to make the Eurozone work. Many don't want that, however, as it would mean a further loss of sovereignty.

What has the euro experiment delivered? It has showcased the power of Germany in Europe, with the strongest economy wielding the greatest financial and political clout. It might have benefited those able to afford an apartment in Berlin, far more than the struggling families in Athens. It's also demonstrated the power of sharing a currency, and how it can bring smaller, poorer members to their knees. It brings home the fact that a currency can be so much more than just what we spend in the shops every day.

∽

Dmitry Sokolov was keen to exchange his dollar for euros, to have his own share of Germany's wealth. He's lucky to have the means to do so. There are many people, all over the world, who would also like to share in Germany's riches – and they will go to varying lengths, via different routes, to achieve it.

The fortunes of the EU clan vary considerably, and incomes in the newly arrived states of the former Eastern European bloc in particular tend to be much lower. An electrician in Germany earns six times as much as one in Romania. The cost of living is higher in Berlin than in Bucharest, but only twice as high. The difference between those earnings and costs represents the standard of living. The possibility of a higher standard in Berlin could well be enough to tempt a Romanian electrician to pack his bags and his diploma and head west. He'd be one of the many European economic migrants gravitating towards the riches of Germany: in 2015, that was 685,000 people. Although many are sending a proportion of their new-found wealth back to their countries of origin, this brain drain has also left a skills deficit back home.

Crucially, visitors such as our Romanian electrician do come with skills. Germany has long been on a quest to ensure it has enough qualified workers. Between 1955 and 1973, it invited 'guest workers' from Turkey and other Mediterranean countries to plug a gap. Today, it may well be Polish plumbers or Romanian electricians who are constructing Dmitry's flat. The greatest demand, however, is for IT workers and engineers, to maintain the manufacturing heartland's cutting edge. For that, Germany has had to look further afield, and it's not averse to the right workers from the rest of the world: as long as they hold a coveted skill, they can apply for a visa.

Slightly less welcome are European guests without a specific high-end skill: the waiters, shop assistants and manual labourers who keep Germany's coffee shops, retailers and building sites running. The stream of willing workers keeps wages down for their employers, but some fear that it also keeps Germans out of jobs, and lowers their incomes, because the newcomers are content to work for lower wages, and possibly do jobs that others are not prepared to do.

However, Germany needs to keep its workforce growing because, like much of the richer world, Germany is getting older.

The term for the way a population evolves as a country modernises is 'epidemiological transition'. In an early stage of development, families tend to have lots of children. Poor medical provision and sanitation might mean some don't survive childhood, and, in the absence of a welfare system, parents need to ensure they're looked after as they age. As an economy develops, living standards improve. More women work outside the home and family planning comes into play; they have fewer children. People may live longer, but a longer, more affluent life brings with it greater threat of diabetes, heart disease and cancer.

The German population is ageing, and already more than one in five Germans are over the age of sixty-five. That's 16 million people who might not be earning or paying taxes any more but who require costly pensions and healthcare. One in every four euros spent by the German government funds the upkeep and care of older people. Keeping a seventy-year-old healthy costs four times as much as it does for a thirty-year-old. By 2040, more than two in five Germans will be over sixty-five. The cost to the public purse will rise faster than the economy can grow. The country needs more taxpayers to foot the bill. People are being enticed to work longer but half a million are still retiring every year, and fewer babies are being born in Berlin's hospitals.

Having one in five of its people over retirement age doesn't rank Germany as simply ageing; it's officially 'super-aged', according to the United Nations. It's not alone: Japan, Italy, Greece and Finland also hold that badge of seniority. There's an urgent need to think about how to ensure there are enough workers to fund the non-workers. The answer might not lie in drafting in other members of the EU. Europe's less wealthy populations are also getting older, although at a slower rate. Other emerging economic firepowers – Brazil and China, for example – aren't far behind. China has been hamstrung by its one-child policy, which was intended to curb the exploding population but has also had an impact on the number of people of working age in the country. Meanwhile, Brazilians are having fewer babies and living longer.

Given this growing economic pressure, the German government welcomes not only the skills of the new arrivals from Eastern Europe but also their taxes. Germany needs in excess of 250,000 arrivals every year, just to keep ticking over. It needs those workers to keep the economy growing, and to support the retired. Other super-ageing economies face the same challenge. Of course, ultimately, even new arrivals retire, and even more young people will be needed to support them. It's a massive conundrum.

So where is Germany to look to keep its worker-bee numbers topped up? The youngest nations are in Africa – Nigeria, for example – or among the Gulf States, including Qatar and Bahrain; or in populous South Asia, including India and Pakistan. Germany isn't averse to a few visitors from these developing nations, as long as they have skills.

Then there are Germany's uninvited guests. In 2015, Chancellor Angela Merkel took the unusual step of opening Germany's borders. A small but sizeable number of the world's people were on the move, in particular fleeing the civil war in Syria. Thousands were making a perilous trek to Turkey, and then across the Aegean Sea to Greece. Chancellor Merkel offered them asylum. People escaping repression or conflict in places such as Iraq or Afghanistan joined them. In 2015, Germany's population was swelled by 1.1 million asylum seekers, a third of them Syrian. The country became a magnet for the world's distressed and dispossessed. It was a compassionate move that offered sanctuary to those in a desperate situation.

At a time when states and trading blocs are guarding their borders and fortunes closely, offering those from far away more than a bed for a night was a controversial decision. Not everyone was convinced. Merkel's policy was labelled 'the biggest foreign-policy mistake any Western leader has made since 1945' by the British anti-EU politician Nigel Farage, and opponents elsewhere in Europe feared this gesture was likely to encourage more people, and not just refugees, to make the journey to Europe uninvited. Those objecting were concerned that economic migrants – those not necessarily persecuted but simply in search of a better life – were also sneaking in uninvited.

This pattern of migration is, of course, nothing new; people fleeing religious persecution in Britain in the seventeenth century appropriated the home of the dollar, the USA. The difference is that there is now a far greater number of people in the world protesting a right to a decent standard of living. The struggle for resources has intensified as populations have grown. And, as long as some countries lag behind others in development, the exodus from poor to rich countries is likely to continue. It's another argument for aid or investment within poorer countries.

In Germany, the migrants bumped up annual population growth to above 1 per cent for the first time in over fifty years. Inundated with new arrivals, German officials struggled to process applications swiftly, sifting out those who'd arrived from 'unsafe' countries – Syria, for example – as opposed to those deemed 'safe', including Albania and Pakistan. They were refusing asylum to the latter, but delays meant it was easier for some people simply to disappear and become illegal immigrants, doing cash-in-hand jobs.

The arrival of more than a million people at its borders sounded the 'stranger danger' alert to many Germans and, as German citizenship equals the right to move around the EU, some of Germany's neighbours were equally uneasy about the situation. Then there was the economic aspect. Some in Germany were concerned that new arrivals, with no claim to Germany's wealth, would be 'living off' the German people, claiming benefits and using public services but giving nothing back.

The reality, many studies in Germany and elsewhere show, is that migrants, on the whole, tend to be as qualified, or more so, on average than the population they're joining. One study from the Centre for European Economic Research showed that in 2012 the 6.6 million people living in Germany with foreign passports paid $4,127 more in taxes and social security on average than they took in social benefits, generating a surplus of 22 billion euros that year. So ultimately, they tend to pay more in to the system than they get out.

'Ultimately' is the key word. It takes time, possibly a few years, for immigrants to become part of the system, both socially and in the labour market. The latest arrivals are different. Historically, most people invited into Germany were selected according to the skills they had. But the single market and the widening of the EU was attracting fewer skilled workers from across Europe. The refugees entering Germany from further afield since 2015 were, on average, less skilled than the migrants that preceded them.

Would the German people, already having to fork out more to look after their own ageing kin, also have to pay to look after these new arrivals? According to the German government, about half the one million refugees arriving in 2015 would be eligible for state benefits. The cost to the public purse, it estimated, would be 10 billion euros in 2016. That's a small amount for an economy that generates trillions in income every year, but it is still not trivial.

And what of the economic effects? It's the workers at the lowest tiers of pay and skills who might feel most threat from the new arrivals. Research by the University of Oxford did show that their wages might be pushed down, on average by a modest 2 per cent. Others highlight that German unemployment, despite the swelling of the population, is not soaring; in fact, the economy in 2017 became a bright light in the West. Merkel's long game was paying off, but only because her economy was growing at a strong enough rate to cope. This is true for all nations: mass immigration can work in financial terms only when an economy is thriving enough to need more workers. Otherwise, the social issues that accompany a large influx can dominate.

Even with a flourishing economy, however, many Germans fear

their own needs are being usurped. They are concerned that this is not the solution for their ageing population; that, in fact, their caring burden might even be increased with the need to provide public services – health and education (and, indeed, benefits) – to new arrivals. Even those with a generous approach to refugees fleeing misery and the threat of death were left uneasy.

Opening up to new economic forces, or to new arrivals that might need to integrate, isn't easy. Yet it may be the key for our economies to keep growing and prospering. For Germans and for migrants, it can sometimes be a struggle to reconcile our day-to-day lives with the great tides that are shifting around us. Those personal experiences differ sharply, as with all aspects of globalisation.

The cosmopolitan melting pot of Berlin is booming. Such a buoyant property market means things are good for the Mitzi apartment block's developer. Business prospers as long as the housing market is flourishing. The company will be responsible not just for its employees' wages but also for some of their taxes and for payments to their pension funds. As the Greeks know, these funds, however abstract they might seem, can make or break economies as well as individual retirements. Dmitry Sokolov is hoping to secure his finances for the years ahead by gambling on Germany's property market. His dollars, which he exchanged via Deutsche Bank, will also be used by someone who shares his focus on life after work, ultimately funding the retirement plans of a worker in Berlin. Whether a building engineer for Mitzi, or a supervisor in a department store, a worker in the city (with their employer) is almost certain to be paying into a pension fund.

That pension fund is run by trustees, with fund managers in Frankfurt managing the pot of money. They have to decide how to grow this fund over several decades so that the engineer can enjoy a comfortable retirement. The fund manager, Hans Fischer, as he does with all investments, has to balance getting the best returns – growing the pot – with safety. He is spoilt for choice, and in fast-moving financial markets, the appeal of investments changes all the time. He has the luxury of investing the cash paid into the fund for many years. Now, however, he's concerned about the value of the euro falling, so he changes some of the fund's euros into dollars, which could help to guard against that risk. If he then uses some of these dollars to buy American investments, they will bring returns to the fund – in dollars. That means he's not only 'insured' against the euro weakening but will also probably get a higher return than if he simply held dollars in cash. So, which American investments to choose, and who to ask for advice?

Hans is not constrained by national boundaries in seeking help. For one very lucrative sector, the closer bonds within Europe have made a huge difference. If a bank or other financial institution has an office in one EU state, it can trade freely with the others. In EU terms this is known as 'passporting'. It means that an American bank with a London base can operate in Budapest or Berlin. And it is London that's benefited the most from passporting. It means choices, lower fees and, of course, bigger profits.

Napoleon Bonaparte is said to have called England 'a nation of shopkeepers'. A couple of centuries on, that still rings true in the UK's capital city. After all, bankers are basically peddlars of investments, selling money to make money. To upscale his dollars into a bigger fortune, Hans picks up the phone and calls London.

8

A bad day at work for the Masters of the Universe

Germany to the UK

Emily Morgan is at her desk by 7 a.m. Coffee in hand, she's avidly scrolling through information on her computer screen, having already devoured the pink pages of the *Financial Times* on her journey on the London Underground. She works on the trading floor in one of the many banks across the financial district. By this time, the air is thick with anticipation, caffeine and the smell of bacon sandwiches.

Hundreds of her colleagues sit at desks in neat rows, multiple screens blinking with rapidly changing data, spewing out updates. They're counting down the minutes until 8 a.m., when London's stock markets open, and pounds – and dollars – will change hands at a rate almost too fast to count. The atmosphere is one of suppressed tension.

Emily is a salesperson, dealing with the bank's customers who have large sums of money to invest. People like her might be acting on behalf of pension funds, or wealthy countries, or other banks.

She's the 'go-between' that links the bank's traders with her clients: in this case, Hans and his pension fund. He and Emily will take the advice of her colleagues – analysts and economists – whose crystal-ball-gazing is intended to unearth the most lucrative investments. Then she passes her order to traders, who, just as in any market, will weigh up supply and demand and inform her of the going price. If that price is right, the deal goes ahead. Entrusted by Hans with 'his' dollars, she's looking to buy some American assets from American banks. Of course, that bank can deliver at the touch of a button, and, as we'll see, there are buyers waiting to snap up that same dollar.

Above Emily's desk, clocks on the wall tell the time in Tokyo, New York, Sydney and Buenos Aires. London is not just Europe's financial capital; it's the world's. It's handily located in the middle of the world's time zones: five hours ahead of New York, nine behind Japan. It's English that's the global business language – for now.

The dollar coming in from Hans is just one of trillions that pass through the City of London every day. Money is the lubricant that enables the global economy to run smoothly, the fuel that keeps livelihoods on track. Managing it is huge business in the UK. Much of the world's money converges on London, and has done through the city's long and distinguished history.

'Sugar and spice and all things nice' is a line from a nineteenth-century English nursery rhyme. It's the answer to the question: 'What are little girls made of?' It could equally describe what lies behind the world's financial system. In 1600, the East India Company was established in London, bringing together merchants who were setting sail around the world in the new age of discovery. The aim was to facilitate the transport and trade of commodities from the Far East, including silk, salt and tea. It was known as a 'joint stock company' because it had multiple shareholders who each owned a bit of the company ('stock') and could profit from its success. Unusually, if the company collapsed, investors weren't liable for the risk; their liability was limited to the value of their share.

Two years later, the Dutch set up their own East India Company. Its shares could be bought and sold to the public in a marketplace: the Amsterdam Stock Exchange. The ability to trade these shares made them more attractive to investors, ensuring the company a supply of funds in order to prosper and grow. London's own stock exchange was founded in the nineteenth century. A far cry from today's trading floors, it had its origins in the city's coffee houses, where genteel gents had already been meeting for many years to consult lists of market prices, and exchange investments. Both East India companies were commercial successes (with Britain's company going on to rule India), and their legacy was to cement the foundations of capitalism and modern finance, the system that powers growth by financing industry.

With the expansion of the British Empire, the City of London became the financial heart of the world, but truly modern international finance in London started in 1986 with a bang – the 'Big Bang' – when the UK deregulated its financial markets. That meant that no longer were shares traded face to face on the floor of the London Stock Exchange by 'open outcry'. Instead, electronic trading became the norm, and the rules over who could trade – and how much they could charge – were softened.

We have technology to thank for fast-tracking the global financial system into the twenty-first century, linking people and funds on a massive, unprecedented scale. The old rulebook was torn up overnight, resulting in more competition. Foreign firms were allowed a greater role in London. Regulations were freed up to a degree that few, except the USA, could match. London boomed as a financial centre. The City had traditionally been a 'Square Mile', hemmed in by the Tower of London in the east and Blackfriars in the west. As the number of financial institutions multiplied, those borders shifted, taking in the old warehouse district of Canary Wharf in the east, and stretching as far west as the aristocratic haunts of Belgravia.

By 2016, the financial industry contributed almost $180 billion to the UK per year, and kept over 1 million people in work. It was by far the most profitable part of the economy, keeping luxury retailers and the top end of the housing market in business and also providing a steady stream of tax earnings for the government. It has meant that London and the south-east boom in a way that the rest of the UK doesn't. It has made a lot of people very wealthy, and skilled banking staff have flocked the world over to make London their home. These days, having a London office is an obvious choice for an American bank, as it can then operate across Europe. The fees and profits these banks earn from dealing with clients abroad count as the UK's 'exports' of financial services.

The Big Bang didn't just change the size and spread of London's banking sector, it also changed the people working in it. By the end of the 1980s, the stereotypical bowler-hat-wearing, briefcase-toting, upper-middle-class gent had been replaced by swaggering youths in striped shirts slugging champagne. The yuppies (young, upwardly mobile people) had arrived. Gone were the austere habits of their parents, born and raised in the shadow of a crippling world war; excess was back in fashion. They were paid megabucks to make uber-megabucks. It was all about the penthouses, the social whirl, the beach houses. Luxury car dealers and yacht brokers couldn't believe their luck.

Over in Wall Street, the swagger was even bigger. These ambitious dollar-chasers were captured in Tom Wolfe's quintessential New York-based novel, *The Bonfire of the Vanities*, as 'Masters of the Universe'. They weren't necessarily from the richest families; the promise of untold riches actually presented a bigger incentive to those from less affluent backgrounds. Greed was suddenly good, to paraphrase the lead character in the iconic 1987 film *Wall Street*, on both sides of the Atlantic. As London modernised and boomed, the new breed of dealer became more diverse – and was more likely to be a woman. However, Emily is still in the minority. Fewer than one in five of those working in front-line jobs on trading floors are women.

With life-changing riches on offer at the top, sharp elbows are needed to get a job and build a career. Emily's aware there are fewer and fewer people moving up the ladder. It's all about the zeros you can add to the bank's balance sheet. The worst performing 10 per cent of staff is regularly discarded without a backward glance. Emily's guarding every dollar she brings in, nurturing the relationship with her clients. Keeping them sweet means steering them towards the most profitable investments, enticing them with innovative strategies and products that beat what's available elsewhere, and making them more money. Emily's job is no different from that of the gentlemen meeting in the City's coffee house in the eighteenth century: to make money out of money.

For the market in money to become established, the concept needed the structures and security of eighteenth-century London (and Amsterdam). Spreading the risk of investment between multiple shareholders was the key innovation. Nowadays, to make it all work, sophisticated regulatory and legal infrastructure is needed, along with international agreement and standards. However, in some ways, we're still in uncharted territory with new frontiers appearing all the time.

❦

Emily has a lot of investment choices to offer that German pension fund, and they've become more intricate and unusual over the years. The vast multitude of investment choices in an increasingly complex global economy is one of the reasons why so many of us don't know what's going on (or even what to do with our own money) – and why, in fact, so many banks and governments themselves have struggled to keep track of it all.

First, she could offer the simple fare, the stocks and shares (also known as equities) – those tiny slices of a company first sold in Amsterdam and London. Nowadays, they are often sold off to investors as part of an IPO – an 'initial public offering', which, as the name suggests, means anyone can buy a little part of a company. For a company, going 'public' like this is a great way to raise a lot of investment money, although it does mean that the company then has to answer to the demands of its shareholders. Tech giants such as Twitter and Google caused huge waves when they launched their shares on the market in this way.

There are a number of small-scale investors who own company shares; in theory, anyone can have a slice. In the 1980s, a politically inspired privatisation of utilities providers in the UK, designed partly to make them more efficient and accountable, encouraged the wider public to hold shares. The idea was to get ordinary people invested and engaged in the financial system, and inspire a sense of entrepreneurship. However, most owners of company shares still tend to be large institutional investors such as pension funds.

A company's market value is the total value of its shares. If this figure is big enough, the company gets a place on the leading 'index' of a country, which lists the share prices of companies that have been offered to the public in this way. In the UK it's the FTSE 100, an index that includes global household names such as Vodafone or HSBC, the 'blue chip' titans. Slightly less gigantic companies make up the FTSE 250 – still largely well known in London, less so internationally. Most countries have at least one index. The USA has the Dow Jones Industrial Average (made up of only thirty companies' share prices), the more tech-heavy NASDAQ composite and the widely spread S&P 500 (covering 500 companies). France, Germany and Japan have the CAC 40, the DAX and the Nikkei 225, while China and India have the much newer Shanghai Composite and Mumbai Sensex. All are a measure of their country's corporate might – or weakness. Like the exchange rate, the index is another way of looking at a nation's economic strength.

Investment managers often offer funds made up of a selection of shares from these indices, a popular and easy choice for investors. They are hoping to make money from the portion of a company's profits paid to shareholders, and are also hoping the value of the shares will increase, so they are worth more in case they want to sell them on.

The shares may change hands many times, and investors buy and sell them for various reasons. Just as in the trading of oil, there are certain 'fundamentals': facts that affect why one share would cost more than another: better than expected profits at the company concerned, for example, or a change of boss. The share price of Walmart can vary with the size of the average customer's basket.

Of course, essential information about a company's performance is not always freely available. Companies know more about how they're really doing than investors do. So, to a degree, investors have to guess. This is an example of what's called 'asymmetric information'. Moreover, even the companies themselves can't predict the future. We can never have perfect information.

More often it comes down to sentiment: a gut feeling about the company's prospects. This might be based on an interpretation of the available facts: for example, a hunch that the latest Walmart store layout is confusing for customers. It might not even be related directly to the company's outlook, but that of the sector or the economy as a whole, or a feeling about the stock market overall.

Investors will also take a bet on what they think other investors will do. This kind of approach has led economists to liken stock markets to a casino, where all the players are trying to guess the other players' next move, and outsmart them. And, of course, those instincts aren't always right. The situation has also been likened to guessing the outcome of a beauty contest, where punters place a bet on which photograph from a line-up will be deemed most popular, not which contestant they personally feel to be the most attractive. And, of course, those instincts aren't always right either.

All this means that markets can diverge from fundamentals and not be an accurate reflection of the underlying state of the economy or of a company. In other words, they're not always efficient.

As in any betting shop or casino, sentiment rules – and that sentiment characterises how the market as a whole is perceived. When investors are optimistic, and shares are generally expected to rise in price, it's called a bull market. But if financial storm clouds have gathered, the bears are said to be out; when a stock market declines by 20 per cent or more over eighteen months, it's labelled a bear market.

Whenever there's a significant wobble in share prices, headline writers love to talk about 'crashes', telling us how much has been wiped off their value. It's one of the most misused and overused clichés in the financial dictionary. A stock-market crash occurs when a market – the FTSE 100, for example – loses more than 10 per cent of its value over two days. It is usually triggered by an economic or financial crisis, which is then inflated by panic. It's an extraordinary seismic shock, leaving its mark not just on investors but also around the world. Examples include the Great Depression in 1929 and the 2008 crash.

More common but still painful is a correction, when share prices drop by 10 per cent over a period of time. That, too, can be triggered by an economic shock, or by investors realising they've been feeling a bit too heady, and it's time to adjust their expectations. A correction normally follows a bubble, which occurs when prices have inflated too far and investors have been carried along on a wave of exuberance.

None of this is new. In 1711, a company was set up that bought the 'rights' to all trade in the South Seas, the waters around South America. Encouraged by the success of the East India Company, whose shares were in scarce supply, investors in London were clamouring for a bit of the South Sea Company and the hitherto untapped riches it promised. Several other ambitious companies sprung up, encouraged by this appetite for shares. Investors hadn't noticed that the South Sea Company, owing in the main to poor management, was over-promising and under-delivering, with ships being lost and cargo rotting. Indeed, it actively encouraged rumours about its success in order to inflate its share price. When this came to light, people realised they'd been paying huge prices for shares that promised little return, and that they'd bought them only because other people seemed to want them. In 1720 the share price crashed and the 'South Sea Bubble' was no more.

Less than a century before that, a craze for a recently introduced, highly prized flower – the tulip – had led to feverish speculation in the Netherlands. Ordinary people poured their life savings into ordering bulbs, believing selling them on would lead to a blooming fortune, because, it seemed, everyone wanted them. But the market crashed, taking the nation's economy with it.

Today, a daily newspaper reader might conclude that nothing good ever comes of share markets, that they're always poised on the edge of freefall. If so, why are our pension funds tied up in them? The fortune of anyone who has a pension – now or in the future – is likely to be wrapped up in these shares. If you have one, you probably own a minuscule sliver of some of the biggest companies, and your future is tied to theirs.

On average, share indices have risen by 7 per cent per year since 1950 in the USA (it will vary elsewhere, depending on the country and its prospects). This is largely because company profits, on the whole, tend to rise – as we'll discover in Chapter 9. In recent years profits and share prices have risen less quickly, which is one reason why pension funds in the West have suffered. However, on the whole, stock markets continue to rise. It's just that 'Shares doing fine, thanks' and 'Billions wiped onto share values today' don't make for such dramatic headlines.

All share markets have a degree of risk, though of course the risk depends on both the country and the company. A younger, faster-growing economy such as India might be seen as having more growth prospects for its companies and shares than a staid old-timer like the USA, though there'll be a greater risk attached. In every country, some companies – such as those producing food, energy or pharmaceuticals – are less impacted by swings in the wider economy, and so less risky. Even in bleak times, people can't completely cease eating, or heating their homes, or treating their ailments. Other types of company are more tied to the swings of the economy. Sales of luxury handbags, for example, are far less likely in a recession. Interestingly, lipstick sales typically rise faster in a downturn; relatively cheap cosmetics provide an instant lift, an affordable touch of luxury even when money is tight.

Weighing up all these considerations, Hans Fischer, via Emily Morgan, could put that pension fund's pounds into British shares. Or he could look at another old favourite, the bond ('gilts' in the UK), as the Chinese government and many investors do. Or he could simply look at currency itself.

There could be a practical reason for a large investor to buy another currency. If Brazil, for example, has a high interest rate, the fund can buy Brazilian currency, and enjoy a higher return from holding that cash in a deposit account there. Switching money like this, from the currency of a country that has a lower interest rate, is known as a 'carry trade'. That cash retains the same level of liquidity – that is, it can be accessed and spent easily. The investor could relinquish a bit of that liquidity for higher returns by investing that money in Brazilian assets – shares or bonds, for example.

For the most part, though, currency transactions in financial markets are driven by sentiment and speculation. Ask a trader what's behind the latest shift in the exchange rate and you might get the muttered answer: 'Arab buying', or 'Japanese selling'. The gusting wind of opinion is everything and it can change direction and speed in a second, depending on what the markets think about prospects for interest rates or growth in a particular country, or even its political stability. Every utterance from a central banker, every bit of economic data, is pored over – as was the case, for example, with the 2014 drop in the Russian rouble.

The old saying about market traders is that they 'buy on rumour, sell on fact'. Being 'ahead of the curve', spotting which way those gusts will be heading and cashing in first is everything. Emotions may be said to drive foreign-exchange markets as much as cold, hard facts. So, like equities, currencies can be said to be operating in a less than efficient market. Traders never know the whole picture about an economy; the information they have is incomplete. That means no one really knows what he or she is buying into when they purchase a dollar, or a pound, or a euro – or even if they're paying a fair price for it.

That all sounds fairly risky – and complex – but those are just the basic staple investments, the reliable old favourites. There's so much more on offer. More adventurous investors may choose to head straight to the section marked 'derivatives'.

The term 'derivatives' covers quite a few different products. What they have in common is that they literally derive their value from something else. They're like the doughnuts of the investment world: tempting but lacking in real nutritional value. They're tools that have been developed to allow investors to make money with their money, but unlike shares, for example, they don't represent an actual investment, or anything concrete at all. In a way, they're just promises – sometimes empty promises.

Take 'options', for example: an option is the right to buy (or sell, but we'll use buying as an example for now) shares, bonds, commodities or foreign currency, at a certain date, at a certain price. You don't *have* to buy them, though: that's the difference from a futures contract such as those used to buy oil, when the buyer is obliged to stump up the agreed price on the agreed day. It carries risks for both sides. The buyers and sellers of options are essentially taking a punt on what they think markets are going to do in the future, and as such they risk making a loss on the trade.

Derivatives were invented originally to reduce exposure to risk, almost like a form of insurance. Take an option, say, to buy several barrels of oil in three months' time at $80 per barrel. If the option is sold for $20, the buyer is protected from the risk of soaring oil prices for the bargain price of $20, and the seller has a guaranteed $20 in her pocket in case the market crashes. Investors are likely to take out multiple bets of this kind on different things, to spread, or 'hedge' their risks. This has become such a precise yet lucrative art that it has led to the explosion of hedge funds. Their managers use meticulous equations and strategy, the rocket-science approach, to squeeze as much money as possible from their trades. They're interested purely in making money, not in the actual assets they're buying, poring over markets and company developments – from takeovers to bankruptcies – to look for money-making opportunities. They're the hardened regular punters who bet on the outcome of every beauty contest, and they can make an awful lot of money doing so.

Derivatives were meant to take the risk out of the market but, in many cases, they're used to speculate, actually increasing the risks. In the great casino, even straightforward options and derivatives weren't exciting enough for the hedge funds, the banks and their more adventurous clients. Many at the start of this millennium wanted to experiment further, so they invented yet more types of derivative. It's a creative business, developing financial instruments sold at the push of a button. They're just equations and numbers on a screen but they can have a huge effect in the real world.

Crucially, two derivatives known as CDOs (collateralised debt obligations) and CDSs (credit default swaps) that were popular among banks at the turn of the century weren't policed. That is, they were not overseen by regulators. This turned out to be a big mistake, as these little poison pills contaminated the whole financial system. Underlying it all was dollars, but not the dollars of a big German pension fund, an arms manufacturer or even an oil producer. They were the dollars of homeowners across America – or, rather, the dollars they didn't have.

Orlando, Florida, lies 4,000 miles across the Atlantic Ocean from London. Its mild climate has attracted many, including Paula Miller, the cousin of our Walmart shopper, Lauren. In 2002, Paula moved to the Sunshine State, but the chill soon set in. Like many across the USA, Paula had been encouraged by low interest rates and lax rules to take out a mortgage, regardless of whether she had a job or any other form of regular income. The lender wasn't interested in checking.

Why was money so cheap and so easy? This is where Alan Greenspan ('The Maestro'), then chief of America's central bank, the Federal Reserve, comes in. In 2001, the US economy was looking shaky, and overseas demand was faltering in the wake of the Asian crisis. Then came the terror attacks of 9/11. The markets plunged, and concerns grew that the economy would as well. The Fed slashed the core rates that banks use to borrow from each other. They were 6 per cent at the start of the year, and just 1.75 by the end. As concerns grew, the rate cuts intensified, and so did the availability of loans. Consumer spending, that linchpin of the economy, roared into life, fuelled by credit. It wasn't until 2004 that those rates were hiked up again, albeit a little too late. Could the Maestro have been asleep on the job, too relaxed about the risks of this easy, cheap credit? As we'll see, most probably. Lurking in the shadows were the ogres that ultimately lay behind the crisis: the predatory lenders who'd funded Paula's dreams, enabled by deregulation and a system that aggressively promoted home ownership.

Meanwhile, Paula, with a home to call her own, was living the American dream. It wasn't just that she owned a house. Its value was rising, so she was feeling richer, and more relaxed about spending. The Maestro had become her fairy godfather.

Lenders were happy, too. They could lend even to those clients who weren't creditworthy but who believed that good times were coming. They'd found yet another way of making money out of them. The mortgage loans – the liabilities held by the bank – were bunched together with mortgages from other states to form a financial instrument, called a 'mortgage-backed security', that could be sold to investors, who'd 'own' the debt in the same way that China owns US debt when it buys government bonds. The debts were bundled together because banks thought it was an effective way of spreading the risk, pooling different types of customers from different states, where there were different demands for housing. Even if the group of borrowers consisted of 'subprime' customers with shaky job prospects, there was less risk of all of them losing their jobs simultaneously than there was of one person doing so.

It was financial alchemy, transforming bricks and mortar into a goldmine. So why stop there? Lenders also bundled in loans for cars and credit-card debt. It was these diverse bundles that made up collateralised debt obligations (CDOs). With these, the seller of a CDO commits to paying the buyer if debtors such as Paula default on their loans. In turn, these CDOs were chopped and changed repeatedly, creating CDOs that were backed by CDOs. As with government bonds, there was no shortage of those wanting to 'own' – or, rather, to underpin – Americans' debts, even if they didn't understand them. America's debt is popular all over the world, all the way to China and beyond. Everyone wants to lend to Americans, or, to put it another way, to own their debt. The US economy is seen as one of the safest bets around.

CDOs offered generous returns to investors, and were perceived as safe – thanks in part to the agencies that are meant to rank these risks, the credit ratings agencies.

Around these CDOs sprang up insurance policies – credit default swaps, or CDSs – which also could be sold on. Emily Morgan and her team could sell them to investors: wealthy countries and pension funds across the globe. Hedge funds saw even more money rolling in. Selling these loans on meant lenders could erase loans from their balance sheets and transfer the credit risk associated with them. That meant they could afford to offer even more loans to homeowners, and indeed they borrowed more funds from other banks to do so. As the thirst for CDOs increased, lenders looked at even riskier prospective homeowners. Overindulgence was the norm.

The complexity of the financial products, in a system that was incredibly opaque, meant that judging risk was impossible. The market wasn't able to act efficiently; it wasn't based on the 'fundamentals'. It was unsustainable.

And so, inevitably, the party stopped. Between 2004 and 2006, US interest rates jumped from 1 per cent to 5.25 per cent, as the central bank tried to temper the rate of growth. It was worried that inflation and the economy were growing at an unsustainable clip. Paula Miller suddenly found she couldn't pay back her mortgage. Demand dried up. The higher interest rate meant fewer people were rushing to take out new mortgages and property prices dropped. People fell behind on their mortgage repayments, and their homes were decreasing in value as no one wanted, or was able, to buy them.

Those sub-prime loans held by investors looked like very bad news. By 2007, there were $1.3 trillion worth of loans to people who weren't creditworthy. The opacity and toxicity of CDOs were exposed. They were increasingly worthless. It turned out that investors didn't really understand how bad a bet Paula – or indeed the Orlando housing market – was. Four out of every ten of her neighbours were struggling to pay off their debts. It was a scenario replicated to some degree across America. Those buying the CDOs had been oblivious to their plight. They hadn't looked too closely, and even if they had, the strands of what they'd actually bought were too complex to unravel.

It was a British bank that sounded the first alarm bells about the crisis brewing across the water. In February 2007, HSBC revealed huge losses at its American mortgage arm. Six months later, French bank BNP Paribas shocked investors when it froze three of its investment funds. It said it couldn't place a value on the mortgage-backed securities in them – because no one wanted them.

If banks didn't know if their own funds were worth anything, how could they be confident about the solvency of their competitors? The financial system thrives by banks lending to each other, making the most of the funds they have. At every level of the economy, both money and credit are a circular system of trust – of faith, essentially – and as soon as it is damaged, it doesn't work.

As the fear and suspicion grew, banks stopped lending to each other, as they weren't confident they would get their money back. Since the whole system was affected, each bank had to hold on to its own money as it wasn't able to borrow from elsewhere.

A 'credit crunch' ensued. Many banks found themselves struggling to cobble together the cash to keep going. Among Florida's biggest lenders during the bubble were Wachovia, Ohio Savings, Washington Mutual, BankUnited, Lydian Private Bank and BankAtlantic. The financial crash would pull them under.

The pain wasn't confined to the USA, of course: banking operates beyond geographical borders. The global chain reaction led to a string of financial casualties. The Royal Bank of Scotland wasn't just one of the world's biggest banks; its balance sheet was bigger, at over $3 trillion, than the UK's entire GDP. The UK finance minister, Alistair Darling, was shocked when the chairman of RBS confessed that the bank was only hours away from running out of cash. A bank makes its money largely from lending but it also has to ensure it has the reserves to pay out to its customers if required to do so. A government bailout was hurriedly arranged.

Banks and institutions across the globe were in equal need of rescue. This wasn't simply using taxpayers' money to save bankers' jobs. These are organisations whose operations affect the fortunes of those far beyond their walls. Ordinary people risked losing their money and homes; the institutions were 'too big to fail'. However, on 15 September 2008, one of Wall Street's biggest, Lehman Brothers, did fail: the 150-year-old bank held mortgage-backed securities that had once been valued at $50 billion. Like

Lehman's share price, those securities were now worth next to nothing.

The snowballing crisis had been triggered by layer upon layer of overvalued yet little-understood derivatives, woven in a complex web around the borrowing habits of ordinary Americans. They'd initially been designed to defend against risk and protect against the downside. Yet derivatives had become speculative tools all too often used to take on more risk in order to maximise profits and returns. In Lehman's case, the result was financial obliteration. Far from being too big to fail, it was too expensive to save.

Governments worked feverishly though 2007 and 2008 to stop the rot. But holes blown in the banking system meant that citizens of London and Orlando were united in anxiety and potential hardship. When anxiety sets in, the economy suffers. People stop spending. As the banks' funds dried up, they stopped lending, withholding dollars from each other and from customers. The panic that infected Wall Street translated into a slump in confidence and spending on Main Street, USA.

It just goes to show that if money doesn't move around the system, everything stops. If people are not willing to spend, trade and lend to each other, activity dries up and economic collapse is the likely outcome.

With fewer dollars circulating, incomes shrank and jobs were lost – especially as, across the West, consumers had previously been able to borrow to fund their spending. Recovery was painful. Five years after the sub-prime crisis in 2012, Paula Miller, like nearly half of all mortgage owners in Florida, was still 'under water'. She owed more than her home was worth, but she was one of the lucky ones. Managing to scrape together enough to keep up with the payments, she at least still had her home. But she was stuck, and she's still angry. Who should she blame?

It was easy to point at those greedy Masters. Alan Greenspan, steering America's central bank, had expected the banks to police themselves. They didn't. Those derivatives had been hard to scrutinise. Credit ratings agencies are meant to monitor and label risk, but they stood accused of being in the pockets of the banks, and turning a blind eye. Banks had also got away with using riskier, questionable and overinflated types of funds to make up the reserves they needed to ensure their solidity. They too saw themselves as 'too big to fail'. When the financial crisis meant the value of those funds evaporated, the threadbare state of many banks' core finances was exposed.

Regulation suddenly became the buzzword across the USA and Europe. Stricter rules were imposed, controlling how much capital banks needed at their disposal to ensure their solvency. Equally, rules were tightened up regarding how much consumers could borrow, or banks lend to them. Consumer creditworthiness was more heavily probed. That might be safer for the banking system but puts the likes of Paula at risk of not being able to afford a new home. Balancing risk with looking after the needs of households can be tricky.

Almost 8 million Americans had lost their jobs by late 2010 as the economy contracted. Even businesses that were household names – including General Motors and some airlines – were running out of cash. The cliché goes that when America sneezes, Britain catches a cold, so great are the links between the two. Sure enough, with its economy shrinking for more than two straight quarters, the UK also entered recession. Joblessness was growing at its fastest rate for almost two decades. The pain spread to Europe and Asia. Even China, as we have seen, wobbled.

By 2010, for most, economic fortunes had begun to turn the corner to some degree. Financial stability returned to the UK and the USA. The economic hangover, however, remained. Concerns were growing about the impact on government funds, as the price of the bailout and the need to support impoverished households became apparent. Instead of giving the latter more help, some governments decided, controversially, to rein in spending to pay off the bills raised by the crisis. Whereas in the UK, for example, this was largely a political decision, in Greece it was more a move to appease the panicked bond markets, to ensure its government could still borrow at a reasonable price. Either way, taxpayers found there was a steep price to pay for the help they and the banks had recently received.

Governments had seen their annual deficits soar. They had to borrow more. The size of the UK government's debt doubled in the wake of the financial crisis. Austerity was the buzzword. To keep their creditors – those bond buyers – happy, governments claimed that they needed to show they had a grip on their finances. It could be argued that public workers saw their pay frozen, partly to benefit investors elsewhere.

Both Emily Morgan and Paula Miller witnessed the crisis at close quarters, but their ensuing fates diverged sharply. Borrowers may have been irresponsible, but a large portion of the blame lay with the lenders who'd preyed on them, and the type of misjudged regulation that allowed that to happen. Bankers did have their knuckles rapped, but their bonuses survived. Meanwhile, the rest of the population felt the effects of sharp cutbacks in government spending. Overall, the UK economy has grown by about 1 per cent per year on average since the crisis, at less than half its previous rate. Recklessness has been replaced by resentment and inequality.

Current and future taxpayers will have to pay the price for traders' gambling and the regulators' benign neglect.

In the UK and across Europe, that sense was heightened further as people from poorer parts of the EU flocked in looking for work. Emily might be doing all right, but many others were suspicious and fearful. They felt their lives were being dictated by bankers and 'Eurocrats' with a different agenda. As the headlines would have it, people wanted to 'take back control'. Those feelings boiled over in a way that would have the world gripped.

On 23 June 2016, almost a decade after the financial crisis erupted, the UK was hit by another seismic wave when 17,410,742 British people voted to leave the EU, outnumbering the 16 million that wanted to stay in. It was a result few had anticipated. Emily Morgan and her colleagues woke up to a future they weren't expecting. Demand for the pound slumped. It plummeted to its lowest level for thirty-one years as investors ran for the safe haven of the dollar.

There were concerns for the future of the UK economy. No one could say, for sure, whether ultimately the UK would be better or worse off. What the markets and the establishment knew lay ahead was extensive short-term disruption, with laborious discussions and agreements to be hammered out in hundreds of areas. The one certainty this vote did deliver was uncertainty over the future. And uncertainty unnerves markets. They may be casinos, full of players who like to place a bet, but those bets are placed on their own terms. The financial system, as we saw with the 2008 crash, is capable of absorbing huge shocks – eventually, and if it gets sufficient government support. However, even though traders are seasoned risk-takers, uncertainty can bring them out in a cold sweat. Faced with unexpected developments, markets can freeze or, worse, panic. Those great tides of sentiment and speculation could punish Britain and its currency if people started to doubt the outlook for the economy, as had happened with Russia.

From the EU's perspective, after the Eurozone crisis, this was the last thing it needed in terms of confidence. For decades, the EU had got used to countries clamouring to join the club, even to share the euro dream. Greece's troubles had led to speculation about whether the Eurozone might be on the brink of disbanding but that soon looked like a minor domestic tiff. The UK, however, had served up divorce papers. As with all shock splits, keeping things civil would be hard. Deeply wounded, the EU vowed to play hard-ball, not least as it didn't want others following the UK's example.

Once those divorce papers were served, once Article 50 had been triggered, in theory the UK had two years to complete negotiations in hundreds of areas. Those kinds of deals take years, even decades, to agree. The trade talks cover everything from the rights of EU citizens living in the UK to the size of the divorce settlement bill to the rules on trading manufactured goods. They cover all industries, from financial services to aviation to agriculture. Under passporting rules, the UK had become the central hub of world finance, the gateway for American and Asian financial institutions to the European markets, the keeper of dollars. Brexit threatened that, with Frankfurt and Paris vying for its business. In the face of uncertainty, Emily Morgan's bank, like many others, might choose an office in Dublin or Amsterdam through which it could continue to access the EU.

If there's no agreement on post-Brexit Britain, the UK has to follow World Trade Organization rules, as it does when trading with other countries. That could mean the return of tariffs, customs checks and quotas, potentially higher prices, and longer waits for imports and for them to get through the border. Of course, divorcing the EU means that the UK is free to look to other trade partners on its own terms. Although it can't start negotiating its own trade agreements until the end of the talks in 2019, in the meantime individual businesses might feel that they can't afford to simply sit and watch from the sidelines. They need to build some relationships of their own. They may be looking westwards: the USA is the UK's biggest single export market in sectors from energy to filmmaking, technology and banking.

Simon Grover works for an ambitious biochemical firm, developing products that improve crop yield. These biochemicals could make a vital difference to big agricultural exporters – such as the USA or India – as they look to feed and profit from a growing population. The firm's headquarters are east of London in Cambridgeshire, in what many call the UK's answer to Silicon Valley. Wary of what lies ahead with Europe, Simon's company is keen to nurture its relationships in the American market. Sales director Simon is packing his bags, off to woo some prospective clients in Texas. So, of course, he's buying dollars.

Buying a dollar in 2017 was a lot more expensive than it had been a year previously, as the pound slumped following the EU referendum. Aware of the risks surrounding the referendum, Simon's company had taken out an insurance policy against the pound falling, entering a contract to buy a fixed amount of dollars at a fixed date, or taken out an option to do so. That kind of hedging contract is taken out by larger companies the world over. In the UK, overall, it meant that there was a delay in the fall in the pound having an impact on price rises for imports on the high street. But these contracts tend to last only a matter of months. After that, companies had to pass on the cost of higher imports or take a hit on their profits. It meant that some months after the referendum, British shoppers were looking at some of the biggest price hikes for over a decade when they bought shoes or a T-shirt.

Simon needs cash, which he'll pick up on arrival. He may feel short-changed, however, thanks to the way the exchange rate has shifted. In 2016, $100 could have cost Simon £65; in 2017, he'd have forked out up to £80. It's a far cry from 2007, when travellers got more than $2 for every £1. The pound that bought him a five-star Houston trip back then would barely stretch to a stay in a dank suburban motel in 2017.

Conversely, a weaker pound makes the UK a bargain for visitors: some 3.7 million visited for an Easter break in April 2017, which is 700,000 more than the previous year. With their money going further, they spent £2 billion on hotels, eating out and shopping, and that was before the traditional summer surge. In contrast, fewer Brits headed abroad.

These are valuable earnings for the UK. Tourism accounted for 9 per cent of UK GDP even before 2016. More visitors mean more demand for the pound. And if weaker sterling equals more attractive British exports, shouldn't that demand push the value of the pound back up? In theory, yes. In practice, we tend largely to keep spending on imports and travelling even if the price goes up; our demand is pretty inelastic, and we simply spend more.

In any case, the currency needed for that kind of trade and tourism actually makes up only a very small proportion of the transactions in foreign currencies that flow electronically through the world's dealing rooms. It's the vast currency transactions that ultimately make a difference, and they're driven by sentiment and speculation. After the EU referendum, investors worried the outlook for the UK was less rosy, making investing there less desirable, and reducing demand for its currency. Cue the slump in the pound. These trades, egged on by constant shifts in sentiment, are the ones that can lead to vast movements in the currency on a daily, or even minute-by-minute, basis.

In the meantime, our – now more expensive – dollar is waiting for Simon in the USA.

9

Feeding the addiction

The UK to the USA

Simon Grover has anxiety over the UK's exit from the EU to thank for the extra expense of his trip, but it's that very anxiety that prompted this particular trip in the first place. Being in the tech business himself, he's already ordered the dollars he needs via his smartphone, ready to pick up at a counter in Houston's airport. The commission charged by businesses when they sell currencies, and the rates they offer, vary widely. Simon could have got his money cheaper elsewhere, but he's prioritising convenience. His dollars will have been purchased by the foreign exchange bureau, ultimately, from Emily's bank. Within twelve hours of departing, Simon has picked up his cash and is checking into one of Houston's many smart, if slightly bland, chain hotels aimed at corporate travellers.

The dollar has come home. In its voyage around the world, passed electronically from one bank to the next, the dollar has distributed income, greased the wheels of trade and prosperity, and shored up the balance of power. Money needs to keep flowing through the system, and that system is global.

Trillions of dollars leave America every year, but trillions arrive, too. This is essential for a large, dynamic, prosperous economy – an open economy that trades heavily and sees investment flow in and out. Business travellers such as Simon are an important part of this activity.

Simon's pile of dollars will quickly diminish, for America is the country of tipping. From taxi drivers to waitresses, an extra 15 to 20 per cent on top of the bill is the norm. A few dollars will eventually be handed over to the helpful concierge at his hotel who's found him a table at the hottest restaurant in town. Her name? Lauren Miller.

Tips are an important source of income for workers such as Lauren because in recent years her wages have struggled to keep pace with the cost of living. Our living standards, how far our money goes, and how confident we feel about our finances will all be influenced by the relationship between wages and cost of living – how high they both are, and the rate at which they rise. America is one of the richest countries in the world, but Lauren's pay slip hasn't been rising as fast as she'd like, or as fast as it has done in previous years. Buying bigger, better – being able to afford the status symbols that typify the American dream – remains just out of reach.

We all expect to keep on getting better off. Economic growth and improvements in living standards are what we've been promised, and aspired to, for centuries. So how can we ensure that constant growth is possible, and with it a rise in our living standards?

There are many things that contribute to our standard of living. First, there are the necessities – food, water, shelter, sanitation and medicine – that enable us to live. Then there are those things that improve our level of comfort: transport and heating, for example. Life expectancy and the availability of refrigerators are often used as markers of the standard of living in a country. In the twenty-first century, of course, particularly in the West, we often measure our standard of living by what we can afford, or consume (that means that GDP per head is the most common barometer of standard of living). The biggest purchase most people will make is a house. Changes in employment patterns and house prices, as well as government spending cuts, have meant that the young these days may be less well off than their parents. A thirty-five-year-old in the UK today is less likely to own a home than someone born in 1900. There's quality of life to consider, too. How much leisure time do we have? Are we healthy? How hazardous is our environment? Can we access – and stay in – education (literacy levels are another indicator)? Those questions are inextricably linked to the standard of living. Health and education may be 'goods' in their own right, but they also affect our ability to earn more – and so spend more.

Though our quality of life is determined by a multitude of factors, we tend to use incomes as a gloss for living standards – because they're easiest to measure (although earning more doesn't necessarily equate to happiness, especially past a certain point). For Lauren, that means her wages.

Ultimately, Lauren's wage is just the price someone is prepared to pay for her labour. And, like all prices, it comes down to supply and demand, which can vary according to what job she's in and where she's working; it can even decide whether she has a job at all.

Supply, in this case, is how many workers there are, and how many have the skills to do the job. The scarcer the skills, the higher the price. Arguably, skilled concierges are easier to come by than a boss who can run a multinational company. Lauren may not feel a Silicon Valley CEO is worth a thousand of her, but the market begs to differ. The fierce competition for medical school or law school means that the average doctor or lawyer is much sought after and, in the USA, generously remunerated.

Furthermore, skills are nothing if no one wants them. If, say, a strong dollar puts visitors off coming to Texas and staying at Lauren's hotel, her bosses are going to feel the squeeze. Pay rises could be smaller; in fact, hotel managers might start to question whether they need so many concierges – or, indeed, any concierges at all.

If the opposite is true, and demand is strong, so too is the need for more workers. In that case, wages have to rise to attract and retain the workers that companies need. If the hotel is constantly fully booked, Lauren's bosses might be able to push up rates for the rooms. They might need more staff. Lauren could find competitors trying to poach her. It's easier to secure a hefty pay rise because her skills become scarcer relative to demand. She – and her colleagues – have more power to get what they want.

What they want are wages that allow them to do well, to have a better standard and quality of life and, ultimately, to buy more. Can they afford to upgrade their phone, for example, or book a nicer holiday? For that, their wages would need to be comfortably outpacing any increase in the cost of living, allowing them to buy more or better.

In a period of inflation, when prices are rising, Lauren's cost of living will be going up.

Central bankers, politicians, even investors the world over seem to obsess over inflation. Inflation is the rate at which prices are rising in the economy overall. The prices of what? Well, of everything. Inflation is measured by looking at a range of items that people typically spend their money on, from haircuts to butter to housing. In other words, the cost of the contents of Lauren's shopping trolley and her other outlays.

Those prices will have been set by different companies for different reasons but, looking at the big picture, prices overall can rise for several reasons. These include demand being very high: people have money and they're willing to spend it, which means retailers can get away with changing the price tag. Or prices can rise if the cost of producing the goods is going up: businesses have to cover higher costs. Or if some important items are in short supply: this could happen with, for example, food, oil or housing. As we saw in Russia, and to a degree in the UK after the Brexit vote, a falling exchange rate can also push prices up overall because it makes imports more expensive.

Governments and central bankers are typically happiest when the annual rate of inflation is around 2 per cent, and we often read about a government's inflation 'target'. It might seem strange for a government even to have a target for inflation. How is it possible for prices to keep on rising forever, and why would that be desirable? Rising prices mean that Lauren's wages have to keep rising to match, if she wants her standard of living to improve. Surely that just makes life more difficult? However, like caffeine or chocolate, price rises aren't necessarily a bad thing . . . in moderation.

Keeping the rate of inflation relatively low helps an economy to grow smoothly. It encourages consumers to spend more (because who's going to wait to buy a new bike next year if it's set to be more expensive then?). As the outlook is bright, companies feel confident about investing in order to expand and produce more.

But if inflation rises too quickly, it erodes the value of the dollar in our pocket and in our bank accounts. That money simply doesn't go as far as it did. Soaring prices can create panic and chaos – just ask those who lived through hyperinflation in Germany or Argentina.

Equally, zero inflation or falling prices (deflation) can lead to a crisis of confidence in the economy's prospects. People put off purchases, as they expect the things they are planning to buy to drop in price in the future, and so companies stop investing. Economic activity slows down, prompting prices to be cut further. A deflationary spiral results, depressing output. Meanwhile, the real value of debts increases. Deflation is poisonous to growth – and having a target of a small amount of inflation each year helps to reduce the chances it will happen.

Maintaining just the right level of inflation is not easy. Policymakers need to keep multiple plates spinning, and pull off precarious balancing acts: they need the multitasking agility of skilled acrobats.

From Lauren Miller's perspective, she'll be looking for pay rises that allow her to keep ahead of inflation, so that she can enjoy a higher standard of living. But how can firms afford pay rises above inflation? If a company's income from sales is increasing only at the rate of inflation – because that's the rate prices are rising by – wouldn't they be losing money if they pay staff more, or even risk going bust?

The company can afford to pay more as long as its profits are going up. Profits are, essentially, the difference between the money earned from sales and the cost of producing the things that get sold. It might sound strange to talk of Lauren 'producing things' but, by being an efficient concierge, going the extra mile for guests, she sets her hotel apart from the rest, enabling it to make more money. She's contributing to its profitability in the same way as a woman assembling a radio in Shenzhen is contributing to Mingtian's profits. In any industry, in any country, increasing profits in part relies on a company's staff being able to produce more at a lower cost. (Selling more also helps.)

Productivity, in its most basic form, is the amount a worker produces per hour. The more that worker churns out, the more the company's cost per unit falls. As a result, its capacity rises. It grows faster and may make more profit. As workers' productivity increases, so the company can afford to pay them more, as long as its products are in demand.

Productivity has become the holy grail of governments the world over, because it enables an economy to grow without damaging levels of inflation. With higher productivity, more goods are produced. They aren't scarce, which means prices aren't soaring. Wages go further, because people have more money to spend, but goods aren't becoming that much more expensive as a result of all that money. There are more goods available, and at an affordable price. Lauren feels richer, and is more prepared to spend her money. Her company is doing well, so it can afford to pay wages that rise as fast, or faster, than the cost of goods.

But surely higher productivity means fewer workers are needed to produce the same number of goods, resulting in fewer jobs overall? In fact, the argument goes that a faster-growing economy needs *more* workers to meet all that extra demand. That means living standards rise. And everyone is happy.

British central banker Andy Haldane set it out bluntly. He pointed out that UK living standards, measured as income per head, have risen twenty-fold since 1850. If productivity had stood still during that time they would have only doubled. Brits would have been stuck in the Victorian age. Instead, more efficient workers, aided by mechanisation and technology, enabled everyone to prosper. Productivity had waved its magic wand. Look at any sustained economic success story, and productivity is key.

Growing productivity basically means giving workers the tools to do the job more quickly, and ensuring they know how to do it.

As fans of the boy wizard Harry Potter will know, magic spells are complex – and far from foolproof. If one core spell existed for growing productivity, it would probably be similar to the transfiguration spells taught to senior pupils at Hogwarts, which transform an object into something else. This particular magic spell might also come under the heading of improving what's known as the 'supply side' of the economy. This is what you need to perform the productivity spell:

1. Technological change: from steam engines to tablet computers, the right equipment can make the job a lot simpler.
2. Having a sufficient number of workers who have the necessary skills – the knowledge of how to do the job, and operate the machinery.
3. Cold, hard cash: investment in new tools and machinery doesn't come cheap.
4. Far-sighted management willing to take the gamble to splash this cash: the payback could be uncertain and might not be evident for some time.
5. A supportive government that creates a friendly environment for investment, and allows for the building of infrastructure from roads to schools and hospitals. (There's no point having a skilled workforce unless they're healthy and can get to work.)
6. Physical and geographical factors: if you're operating a coal-mine, you need a rich seam of coal to start with.

So far that's a pretty comprehensive list of what you need to supply your goods. But for alchemy to happen, the right catalyst is needed:

7. A predictable, rising level of demand to spur the productive process and make it viable.

Assemble these, sit back and hope for the best. From China to Germany, the economic 'miracles' of the last hundred years have productivity to thank. Hauling workers from the fields to the city to churn out manufactured goods for the West meant that China's productivity rapidly increased as it embraced industrialisation. China's economy grew by over 8 per cent per year on average from 2008 to 2013. However, switching the emphasis away from exporting in the last couple of years has seen that rate of growth tail off. Some people wonder if that could hamper China's ambitions for its economy to become the richest on the planet. In Germany's case, strong productivity growth meant that the economy could grow fast enough to absorb migrants without unemployment shooting up.

Assembling all these factors at the same time, getting the mix right, is far harder than it sounds. And it takes time. As any of those 'miracle' countries will confirm, no economy becomes a star performer overnight. As J. K. Rowling, Harry's creator, warned, transfiguration is 'very hard work . . . you have to get it exactly right'. In other words, the transformation takes careful planning, patience and precisely the right combination of both demand and supply. It's easy for it to go awry.

Since the 2008 financial crisis, something odd has happened in most rich countries, especially in the USA and the UK. Productivity growth has slowed right down. In some cases workers have appeared to be less productive. After the crash, the upturn was characterised by rapidly increasing numbers of jobs, which meant an overall increase in output. However, productivity growth – and wage growth – remained very subdued (and, as we'll see, much more subdued than the growth in profits). What was going on? Has Lauren Miller been asleep on the job?

No one's quite figured out this productivity slump, but the answer could lie with company bosses. When the crisis hit, some decided it was easier to ride it out with the staff they had, rather than laying people off, especially where contracts on hours were flexible, and workers relatively cheap. In the late twentieth century, there was much concern at the rise of 'McJobs' (named after the hamburger chain) – low-skilled, lower-paid jobs in booming areas such as retail and hospitality, which made up the bulk of new jobs created in the West. Critics queried – and they still query – how much value they add to the economy. In addition, the aftermath of the crisis saw the rise of the zero-hours contract – lower paid, and with fewer guaranteed hours and perks (sick pay, training, etc.) than its predecessors. This has coincided with the rise of the internet giants – such as Amazon – and the 'gig' economy, represented by the likes of the taxi app Uber or food delivery giant, Deliveroo. These jobs promise lower costs for employers and more flexibility – largely, again, for employers.

Even when the good times returned, many companies opted to rely on relatively cheap labour. Caution made many employers wary of investing. They continued to delay investment in, say, new computers or more efficient cleaning equipment – tools that would help their workers to be more productive. Fresh from witnessing the financial crisis, employees were relieved just to have a job, even if the trade-off was lacklustre wages and uncertain hours. Of course, some organisations did downsize, piling more of the burden on fewer employees to get the work done. But they're actually in the minority.

In recent years, fears have grown that the way capitalism operates in the twenty-first century has hurt productivity growth. Companies are increasingly working at the behest of shareholders. While large pension funds are looking for steady growth in their investments over many decades, many other shareholders may have their eye on the short term, chasing a quick win and maximising the dollars they get back. Investment – a big outlay for a company, the rewards of which may be reaped only through better productivity in the long run – could become deprioritised. Another recent development is the growth of private equity funds, which represent big investors and directly invest in companies, or even own them outright. Their focus – an even more clinical approach – is on cutting costs and getting fast results.

The result of all this is that, post-crash, there are more jobs, but they're less productive and not as well paid as in the past. Normally, a rise in employment means higher wages, because it means employers really need those workers and are fighting to recruit and keep them, but this time that's not the case.

In recent years this productivity puzzle has confounded economists and governments. Lauren Miller's central bank, the Federal Reserve, aims for prices to rise by about 2 per cent per year – its inflation target – because this should represent an economy that's growing at a healthy but not unsustainable pace. It reckons that's consistent with productivity rising by about 1.5 to 2 per cent per year, which means wages should rise by about 3.5 to 4 per cent per year.

In recent years, neither of these things has happened. The average American's pay packet has grown by between 2 and 3 per cent per year since 2007. That's only 1 per cent faster than prices have been rising. So Lauren has been breaking even, but not much more. The situation is worse in the UK, where real wages, after allowing for the cost of living, fell by 10 per cent in real terms in the six years after the financial crisis. In Europe, only crisis-hit Greece could equal this drop.

One issue compounding the productivity puzzle is the thorny problem of how to measure productivity. It's effectively the amount of output compared with the number of people needed to achieve it. But how to measure output? It's easy enough in manufacturing, where we can count the number of cars rolling off production lines. Measuring the volume of crops from rural fields, or the pace of skyscrapers popping up on the Houston skyline, is simple. In some parts of the service sector it's easy to record how many customers get through the checkout line in Walmart in an hour, or how many trims and blow-dries a hairdresser can manage. But how can Lauren's productivity be measured? Is it the number of insider tips she can give guests? The number of mentions she rates in guest satisfaction surveys? This highlights one of the main problems of measuring productivity: it focuses on measuring quantity of output per head, which can be hard enough to quantify, but also it doesn't take account of quality.

The bean counters charged with measuring these things do their best, but the landscape's always changing. For example, in banking, the aftermath of the financial crisis brought with it new layers of regulation and scrutiny. That required hordes of new compliance staff to be added to the payroll. On the face of it, more employees with the same output equals lower productivity. But these people are there to ensure the final product is better, safer and ultimately more efficient and fit for purpose. Then there's technology, the rapid march of which has made it hard for the statisticians to keep up. While investment has been thin on the ground in much of the Western world, where it has occurred – for example, in banking or construction – it has undoubtedly made for greater efficiency. It might mean that actually workers are more productive than official statistics suggest – but we're still not reaping the rewards.

In short, productivity is seen as the magic wand to increase growth and living standards, but it can be elusive, and no one is quite sure how to find it, or what it should look like. And even when productivity is increasing, the outcome can be uncertain: wages don't necessarily keep up.

In the USA, between the end of the Second World War and the early 1970s, each dollar's worth of productivity growth translated into an extra dollar of pay. However, since then, real pay growth slipped. Workers have not seen all the gains of their own increased efficiency. The arguments over why this is the case would fill another book. But, in short, the relationship between productivity and living standards can be changed by a shift in power between workers and bosses. That might mean higher profits for a company don't equal higher pay for its workers. The share of GDP, the nation's income, going to workers is lower today than it was forty years ago. In 2016, the bosses of America's biggest companies earned almost 300 times as much as their average employee. In 1965, that figure was just 20 times. Since the financial crisis, newspapers have heralded more than one 'shareholder spring' in the USA and UK – that's where big investors such as pension funds have voted against big rises in 'fat cat' bosses' pay. But their efforts have been in vain: the gulf between the boardroom and shop floor has continued to widen.

In good times, when agreeing pay rises, bosses will look at how fast inflation is rising, and add a bit on to that. How much might depend on how 'strong' demand in the labour market is, how desperate the need to attract staff. These days, workers appear to be wielding less power. That power depends partly on whether there's a trade union that can add its weight to wage bargaining or threaten strikes. Of course, a union might be able to secure a pay rise for its members even if profits aren't rising. That higher pay could incentivise workers to be more productive. But, if not, these gains are likely to be short-lived. The company will have to lay off workers or go bust. Union power has deteriorated somewhat in the West, and a loosening of regulation can make it easier to employ workers on those zero-hour contracts.

The emphasis on providing shareholders with growth, dividends and profit could have come at the expense of the workers. This is increasingly true with the rise of multinational companies, who might be owned by private equity funds or foreign shareholders and be less likely to have an interest in raising local living standards. Equally, in a competitive marketplace, many companies are pushing work overseas, outsourcing to cheaper workers in places such as India. Alternatively, they may set up bases in countries where tax rates are lower. Dublin has been hugely popular with tech giants for that reason. Employees could be paying a price for the way in which technology and our financial system have transcended national borders.

Ordinary Americans' living standards aren't rising as quickly as they would like, or as quickly as the economy is growing.

Somewhere along the line, the transfiguration spell has failed, due perhaps to a lack of private investment, to government policy or to the availability of the right types of jobs and workers. Even where there are gains from productivity, from increased technological efficiency, a diminishing share of the spoils is reaching workers' bank accounts. The current technological transformation, the Fourth Industrial Revolution, means we can download a movie in seconds, or talk to friends on another continent face to face. But is it making us all richer? Perhaps it has transformed the quality of our life more than our standard of living. It could be an example of 'winner takes all', where only the elite are placed to take financial advantage of technological advances, while others see their wages stagnate.

This is leading to a lot of unsatisfied workers who are watching prices rise around them and not seeing their personal lot improve. We expect living standards to go up, and they can if productivity rises, but that is not what we're seeing at the moment. It matters not just morally or politically but economically as well. If workers have less to spend, then demand in the economy shrinks overall. If productivity is to rise, there needs to be demand to give production a push.

Lauren Miller is happy to have her job, even though she'd like more money for doing it; the tips from customers such as Simon Grover help. The US government is also pleased that Simon has come to visit, bringing dollars with him; any country wants at least as much money coming in as going out. Lauren has earned that dollar, and now she can spend it. And if there's one thing the government wants, it's to make sure that Lauren keeps spending, even if the radio she buys is made in China rather than in the USA.

Consumer spending powers growth, making up the majority, typically 60 per cent, of GDP in modern economies. If producing goods and improving productivity is the supply side, our spending provides the necessary balance: the demand. American consumers are particularly powerful. Together, their outlay accounts for one-sixth of the global economy. But wherever we are, and whatever our income, we're more reluctant to spend if we're uncertain about conditions now or in the future. Confidence is key. Our job prospects, the value of our home, even the political environment can affect how strong – or not – that feel-good factor is. It also depends, of course, on how much money we have in our pockets. Perhaps if Lauren had to pay less tax she would feel richer, and have more to spend?

The IRS (Internal Revenue Service) is the 'most feared agency in America'. One in every $5 of GDP produced in the USA goes to Uncle Sam, that is, the federal government. It comes from, for example, levies on company profits, goods sold in shops, income or other taxes. One-third of that IRS revenue comes from income taxes paid by Americans such as Lauren Miller, and she'll be paying even more in state taxes, to her local government.

Of course, not everyone has an equally straightforward relationship with the taxman. There are some who are seen as not footing their share of the bill. They come in several guises. Some keep their heads down because their income has come from illicit sources: drugs or prostitution, for example. Others evade taxes by squirrelling away cash from legitimate businesses, such as some of those Russian oligarchs buying homes in Cyprus. That's illegal. Or, as the 'Paradise Papers' revealed, there are rich individuals

– such as U2 singer Bono – who are able to afford accountants and complex offshore schemes that result in a lower tax bill. That is legal, unless those schemes have been designed solely to facilitate tax avoidance, which was the case with a scheme for investing in loss-making films, promoted as allowing investors to write off their losses against their tax bills. In the avoiders' club we might also find multinationals – Amazon and Facebook among them – who (legally) claim to be based in countries with lower tax rates in order to minimise their bills. They tend to justify their position by pointing out that they create a great many jobs filled by employees paying taxes.

Whether avoiding taxes (legal) or evading them (illegal), the results are the same. It means less cash raised for government spending, which most often covers what the private sector can't or won't provide. The most obvious example is public goods: something from which no one is excluded, and where one person's use doesn't prevent another enjoying it, such as clean air or defence. Then there are quasi public goods, which don't fully fit the definition of pure public goods. These might include public parks or roads (where congestion could keep everyone from using the latter). For these goods, in theory, everyone benefits, so everyone should pay. If only some pay, but everyone is able to take advantage of them, there'd be a 'free rider' problem.

Then there are those things that ought to be available to everyone regardless of individual circumstances or desires. They have a 'social benefit' that exceeds their private benefit. This includes provision for education and health. Training a doctor, for example, benefits society as well as providing that person with a higher income. What form these social goods take and how they're funded is matter of constant debate. The UK has taken great pride in its taxpayer-funded National Health Service, but some Americans baulk at the idea of subsidising the cost of other people's ill health. They prefer to pay insurers on the basis of their own circumstances.

Governments might also decide to use some of their cash to provide a safety net to those out of work or sick or in old age, redistributing income across the nation. Taxes can also be used to influence behaviour, or to influence markets: those tariffs on Chinese goods, for example, which will make people less likely to buy them.

Decisions about what a government taxes, how much, and what it spends those taxes on depends on political outlook. Americans pay over 25 per cent of their GDP to tax but their competitors across the water in Europe pay on average 34 per cent. The USA, with its relatively low tax burden, has traditionally been much more of a 'free-market' economy, because some feel too much taxing and spending makes the economy less efficient, and reduces choice and consumers' control over their fortunes and destines.

Lowering taxes to help out in tough economic times is a standard tool used by governments. It's a quick, direct way to give people more money, but what if that means the government then can't provide the essentials that help boost productivity? India, for example, needs taxes to spend on essential infrastructure.

However, some have argued that less tax should mean the government makes more money overall. Back in the 1980s, America actually reduced its tax rates with this aim. It was all down to an economist called Arthur Laffer, a favourite of President Reagan. He argued that, up to a point, higher tax rates will bring more money in. But past a certain point, he said, Lauren and her colleagues would be disincentivised from working. Maybe they'd decide to move abroad, or work fewer hours, or hide their tips from the taxman. Higher tax rates could mean a smaller tax take, fewer incentives for the American people to be entrepreneurial and grow their economy. The Laffer Curve, a hump-shaped relationship between tax rate and tax revenue, was born.

Did it work? The Reagan administration slashed the income tax rate for the highest earners from 70 per cent to 28 per cent. Income tax receipts rose from $517 billion in 1980 to $909 billion in 1988, faster than incomes rose during that time. However, that period also saw an immense clampdown on tax loopholes and dodgers. So it is hard to know if the increase in tax take was down to lower tax rates.

All of this was overshadowed by a tripling of the total stock of government debt over the Reagan era. The Republican president may have been a fan of low taxes but he wasn't exactly thrifty. He spent more, relative to America's income, than most of his predecessors. The Cold War didn't come cheap; even the initial bill for his 'Star Wars' missile defence system ran into many billions. That period is remembered for cementing America's position as a nation dependent on others to provide the funds the government needed. The Laffer Curve, meanwhile, remains a subject of heated debate.

How much governments tax and how much they spend used to be an important way to influence economic activity as a whole, though it has fallen out of fashion. Back in the 1930s, British economist J. M. Keynes espoused the use of 'fiscal policy', the tweaking of taxes and government spending to control demand in the economy. That, it was thought, was one way of hitting a desired growth rate.

Want to give the economy a kick-start? The government can spend more, which means there's more money moving around the economy. For example, a big infrastructure project paid for by the government will give people jobs, so they have more to spend, and ultimately it will help boost productivity. Alternatively, it can cut taxes to put more money directly into the pockets of Lauren Miller and her fellow workers.

Want to cool the economy down, if prices are rising too fast, to ward off the dreaded inflation? Turn down the flow of government spending, so there's less money around. Or put higher taxes on the goods in shops, for example.

The use of fiscal policy was all the rage in the 1950s and 1960s as a way of managing economic activity. Then came those oil price shocks of the 1970s and faith in that system dissolved. It was seen as a blunt tool, with unpredictable outcomes. Changes in tax and spending took time to filter through, and it was unclear how much adjustment was needed to remedy problems. It was expensive, too, as it often meant governments had to borrow a lot when they wanted to spend more. That's OK, as long as the economy is growing fast enough to compensate.

But the hike in oil prices caused prices to jump and activity to slow in oil-importing countries. It also led to the creation of a new economic term: stagflation, meaning both stagnant growth and high inflation. This left fiscal policymakers stumped. Their tools of tax and government spending couldn't tackle both problems simultaneously. By the twenty-first century, targeted 'fiscal fine-tuning' had fallen by the wayside. In previous decades, governments might have been expected to react to the financial shocks of 2008 by spending more, which would have given anxious households a boost. Indeed, some argued, along Keynesian lines, that spending more would stimulate growth and incomes, ultimately bringing in more tax revenue. That could ease the government's shortfall, its deficit.

Instead, facing huge bills from bailing out the financial system, many governments took the alternative ideological route and embarked on lengthy austerity programmes. Instead of a safety cushion, some public employees faced wage freezes, while public services were cut.

The emphasis was on cutting the size of public debt. Why? It was all about proving to lenders, those holders of bonds – such as the Chinese government, or the German pension fund – that these governments were still creditworthy. They also argued that the interest payments on these debts were a burden for current – and future – taxpayers. Governments in debt are beholden to their creditors – and that's not just the third-world countries whose debt is such a huge issue. Whether it's because of crisis, misman-agement or the demands of a growing, ageing population, many governments the world over see their debt as a chronic headache.

After the crash, some Americans might have felt that the excesses of bankers had cost them their homes. Now they were paying a further price as governments withheld their dollars. But if governments in debt can't or won't spend to help out, what can they do?

Give people more money.

There are other ways to put money in people's pockets. From the 1970s onwards, 'monetary policy' became the fashionable tool to control Lauren Miller's spending and activity in the economy as a whole. As the name suggests, it's to do with how much money there is, and its price. The price of money is measured by how much it costs to borrow money. And that's all about interest rates.

The key interest rate for any country tends to be the rate at which the central bank lends to other banks, or banks lend to each other. In different countries this could be decided either by the government itself or by the central bank. This rate dictates how much can be lent to households and businesses, and what interest rate they will pay for the loan.

Manipulating the price of credit, and the reward for saving, is a powerful tool. The biggest source of debt for many people is their mortgage. How much they have to spend on those repayments in particular will affect how much they have left to spend elsewhere. Equally, if saving money doesn't offer a good return, people might not bother, and choose to spend it instead.

When times are hard across the economy, interest rates will be set lower by the authorities. For Lauren, the main impact is on her mortgage. A lower mortgage rate gives her more spare cash to play with; she might even be enticed to borrow more, which in turn would boost her spending. Businesses should be persuaded to invest more, as their money isn't earning as much if it sits in the bank, and the possible rate of return on an investment looks more attractive. Governments have to pay less to borrow, so they don't have to raise taxes by as much.

The opposite happens when the government wants to cool down the economy. People are spending a lot, which leads to higher prices and rising inflation. Interest rates go up, which makes it more expensive for people to borrow, so they have less money overall. They borrow less, and they pay more interest on the loans they do have. This encourages them to save more and spend less.

Monetary policy tackles inflation largely by working on the overall demand in the economy. Meanwhile, the costs of production (the supply side) can be kept down by tinkering at company level to improve productivity, or by taxing and spending in order to build infrastructure. Many other factors behind inflation, such as oil prices or a weaker exchange rate, lie largely outside policymakers' control. These factors may reflect global changes and, as we've seen, they can be volatile. It is a perennial headache. On the other hand, the rise of cheap imports from China, for example, has helped to keep prices down without the need for higher rates.

Just as it's not easy to improve productivity, using monetary policy can be difficult in practice. It's not an exact science. Knowing when to change rates, and by how much, is tricky. The eventual impact is hard to gauge, as is the time it will take. It's full of risks and the outcome can be unpredictable. Get it right, and the economy receives a fresh lease of life. On the other hand, any misjudgement can be deeply damaging. This is the policy system used almost universally in major economies in the twenty-first century, so, of course, it was the first lever the central banks pulled when the financial crisis hit. They read from the same playbook they'd been using for decades and cut interest rates. It was a well-rehearsed move, but the scale of it was breathtaking and unprecedented.

In early 2008, the Federal Reserve reduced the key interest rate it charged banks to borrow to almost zero. Many other countries were moving in the same direction. It was a sign of the massive blow to the global financial system, and the action needed to stop it torpedoing the fortunes of people in the West. But it was feared that this still wouldn't be enough to rescue those worst affected by the crunch and ensure that they still had a job to go to and money to put food on the table.

How about simply giving people more money, so that they can keep spending? Although the Bank of England and the Federal Reserve are in charge of printing money, they aren't allowed just to print more and give it away. They can't just create a magic money tree. Or can they?

They can in fact create more dollars or pounds (electronically, at the touch of a button). Central banks can create cash (or reserves) for commercial banks at will – and that's exactly what they did. With those reserves, commercial banks are also able to create money, by extending credit. They have more funds to lend, more cheaply, to more people or businesses – boosting growth and jobs. The central bank can also buy government bonds (and other assets, in some cases) from banks or institutions such as pension funds. As the sellers of those bonds have more cash, they are able to invest further in shares and other funds. The increased demand for bonds will mean lower interest rates, which filter out to the rest of the economy too.

This process is known as quantitative easing, or QE. When it was put into practice after the 2008 crisis, it was unconventional and largely untested, and so hugely experimental. No one knew if it would work or how long it would take. Adding so much money to the economy too quickly could be risky. There might not be enough goods or services to spend it on, meaning it could ultimately just push up prices sharply. But the desperate governments of the West were prepared to pour cash into this massive gamble.

Between 2008 and 2016, the US government poured $3.7 trillion into QE; the Bank of England spent more than £400 billion, or around $600 billion. More direct means were also employed: billions of dollars were pumped into economies via tax cuts or spending boosts. In a time of crisis, governments were resorting to Keynesian measures. But that approach was to be short-lived.

The effects were slow to materialise, and so were hard to monitor. Governments were pulling together to try to protect their millions of people, but they were feeling their way in the dark. However, growth on both sides of the Atlantic did sputter back to life, bringing jobs with it. Not only had bankers, including Emily Morgan, hung on to their jobs but many more jobs were created across the board – albeit typically lower-wage, less secure jobs. The financial crisis in the UK had the distinction of being one of the sharpest downturns and having the slowest recovery on record.

Had throwing money at it been the answer? Who actually benefited? Paula Miller – or Emily's bank? It's hard to know what would have happened without the injection of QE, but the Bank of England estimates the first £200 billion of injections boosted spending – the value of the UK economy – by up to 2 per cent. So it had provided an economic cushion of about £30 billion (around $40 billion).

Where had the additional £170 billion or so gone? It went straight into the hands of the pension funds and investors Emily dealt with and into her bank. It had gone into the financial system, fuelling more demand for shares and bonds, pushing their prices up, and earning financial institutions and their employees more profits and commissions. Central banks had matched the wild bets that led to the financial crisis with a gamble of their own, and the banks had largely cleaned up the spoils. Most gamblers know the odds are stacked against them, but in the casino of the financial markets, those placing an ill-judged bet can still find themselves quids in.

The Bank of England calculated that QE had added 26 per cent to share and bond markets. A strong stock market should be good for general confidence, injecting a little feel-good back into the economy and encouraging spending. But few of the population actually own many shares; much of that wealth belongs to the richest 5 per cent. So the vast majority of households may not have benefited directly from QE. What they did get depended on the spending of Emily and her colleagues, and of wealthy shareholders. What they spent in shops and restaurants, on property or on holidays, boosted the incomes of others. This is the so-called trickle-down effect. However, it didn't necessarily help, because the rich are more likely to save or invest their cash, rather than spend. The New Economics Foundation estimates that, in total, the richest 10 per cent of households got between £127,000 and £322,000 from QE. That 'cheap money' may have gone towards inflating further bubbles, for example in the stock market, or even the top end of the housing market.

What of the overall housing market? Many areas of the USA have seen property values, particularly in the major cities, recover to above pre-crisis levels. The average British home is 20 per cent more expensive than it was in 2007. That home now costs six times as much as the average Brit earns in a year. Forty years ago, a house buyer would have had to shell out only three times as much as they earned. There's a similar, albeit less marked, pattern in the USA. On the whole, house prices have risen faster than incomes over that period, owing to demand outpacing house building, and a wider availability of credit. It means that home ownership is increasingly out of reach. British thirty-five-year-olds are less likely to own a house than their grandparents were at the same age. And when they do, they're having to take on far more debt. But for those who managed to buy a property some time ago, those soaring values mean an increasing amount of wealth is tied up in bricks and mortar. It's an issue leading to an inequality of wealth between the generations across the West.

Demand just keeps on rising in desirable areas, despite more cautious lending since the crisis, while house-building fails to keep up. Ten years after the crash, house prices in London were twelve times the average wage. However, low interest rates have meant that once buyers are on that property ladder, it's relatively affordable to stay on it – at least for now. Mortgage payments now take up a smaller proportion of income in the USA and UK, on average, than they did thirty years ago. But higher interest rates could change that.

The legacy of the financial crisis includes more regulation, and more inequality. The spoils of QE, it could be argued, have not benefited the population as a whole. It was the dependency on cheap ready money – credit by another name – that had fuelled the chaos, yet the medicine dished out to cure borrowers after they'd overdosed on borrowing was yet more credit, more money. The cure didn't neutralise the drug; it just fed the addiction. The credit bubble had burst but governments couldn't afford to stop it reinflating.

A decade on from the crisis, the scars are still clear. The level of debt owed by households has reached new highs. Across America, forms of unsecured credit from plastic to car loans have boomed. The financial crisis failed to dent those appetites. Rather, the low interest rates used to patch up the aftermath of that crisis have encouraged more of the same. The thirst for dollars remains strong. The difference, however, is that the financial system is now subject to more safeguards, meant to ensure that such a crisis could (or rather should) not erupt again.

What links governments, consumers and businesses all over the world? Debt.

The cycle of living beyond our means continues. Apart from a disruption such as a big crash, or a major war, we need to keep spending and producing if we are to improve our lifestyles and sustain the economy, to work the magic of productivity and achieve better living standards in the future.

Consumers' dependency on borrowing is old news for central banks. That's why they rely on monetary policy. But that consumer behaviour has to be understood in minute detail in order to know what changes are needed to get the economy to its desired state. It does not always follow the expected, rational path. If it did, the jobs of central bankers and forecasters would be far easier.

Lauren Miller, like many, finds the contents of other shoppers' trolleys, what they spend their dollars on, fascinating. She can while away time in the checkout queue imagining what they reveal about each shopper's back story. Economists, equally, find consumers' habits as a whole fascinating. Both the amount they spend and what they spend it on have far-reaching implications. The dollars in their hands can control an economy's fate.

Across America – and way beyond – those decisions determine how much of which goods and services ultimately will be produced. That in turn determines where workers are needed, and what they should be producing. What results is known as the circular flow of income. In fact, with American consumer spending totalling one-fifth of the world's GDP, it's more a circular tidal wave. It's a wave made up of dollars, sweeping from consumer to producer across the globe and back again.

These days, many consumers in the West are borrowing to spend, and often what they're spending on is cheap imports. That cheap borrowing is funded, in part, by China and others lending money to America. Everyone wants – needs – Lauren to keep spending: the US government, the Chinese government, investors and pension funds worldwide. Everyone keeps lending in the belief that things are always going to keep getting better, that profits will keep rising, that the productivity spell will keep working. Debt, and faith, bind them all together.

By picking up that radio in aisle 17 of Walmart, Lauren was complicit in maintaining the wave of income that circles the globe. As she stepped through the automatic doors of that air-conditioned retail temple, her aim was to shop. She was playing her own small part in the global system, helping to ensure that men like Wang Jianlin see their fortunes and power rise, and that America's economy can affect those seemingly unconnected, many miles away, such as Dennis Grainger. For now, history, trade, politics and an entrenched financial system ensure it's the dollar that dominates – wherever in the world you are.

Further reading

The financial crisis not only transformed the way our opaque financial system worked, it required those managing the system to make its workings more transparent. Central bank websites (e.g. www.bankofengland.co.uk) have many accessible guides to QE and the like.

The World Economic Forum (www.weforum.org) also publishes topical articles on issues shaping our economy today, from migration to cybersecurity.

In addition, readers may find the following, which cover a breadth of views, of interest.

General economics
Economics: The User's Guide by Ha-Joon Chang (London: Pelican, 2014)

How America became great – and whether its day is over
The Rise and Fall of American Growth: The US Standard of Living Since the Civil War by Robert J. Gordon (Princeton: Princeton University Press, 2017)

Liar's Poker by Michael Lewis (London: Hodder & Stoughton, 2006)

The Big Short by Michael Lewis (London: Penguin, 2011)

'The Global Role of the US dollar and its Consequences': working paper from the Bank of England (www.bankofengland. co.uk/-/media/boe/files/quarterly-bulletin/2017/the-global -role-of-the-us-dollar-and-its-consequences.pdf)

The rise of China
Factory Girls: Voices from the Heart of Modern China by Leslie T. Chang (London: Picador, 2010)

Avoiding the Fall: China's Economic Restructuring by Michael Pettis (Washington, D.C.: Brookings Institution Press, 2013)

The financial crisis: causes and lessons
Other People's Money: The Real Business of Finance by John Kay (New York: PublicAffairs, 2016)

Between Debt and the Devil: Money, Credit and Fixing Global Finance by Adair Turner (Princeton: Princeton University Press, 2017)

How Do We Fix This Mess? The Economic Price of Having It All, and the Route to Lasting Prosperity by Robert Peston (London: Hodder & Stoughton, 2013)

The pitfalls of free markets and inequality
Rewriting the Rules of the American Economy: An Agenda for Growth and Shared Prosperity by Joseph Stiglitz (New York: W. W. Norton & Company, 2015)

The Shock Doctrine: The Rise of Disaster Capitalism by Naomi Klein (London: Penguin, 2008)

What lies behind the decisions we make

Nudge: Improving Decisions About Health, Wealth and Happiness by Richard H. Thaler & Cass R. Sunstein (London: Penguin, 2009)

What the future might look like for the UK and the EU

Making a Success of Brexit and Reforming the EU: The Brexit Edition of The Trouble with Europe by Roger Bootle (London: Nicholas Brealey Publishing, 2017)

Acknowledgements

Like all books, this one has been an almighty group effort, and I'm extremely grateful to all those who've lent their time, thoughts and encouragement along the way.

Huge thanks to the brilliant and ever-patient team at Elliott & Thompson, in particular Jennie Condell and Pippa Crane, for their ideas, taming my inner nerd and enabling my flights of fancy to take shape on the page. To Emma Finnigan, my talented publicist. And to my agent, Mary Greenham of Newspresenters, for her unfailing support, sage advice and good humour.

I am very proud that the team behind this book has been predominantly female, not least as women are still woefully under-represented in the world of economics. However, I'm privileged to have worked with and been supported by some of the most talented men in the industry during my career. In particular, I'm grateful for the encouragement from Roger Bootle, then chief economist at HSBC, and Jeff Randall, former BBC business editor and Sky presenter, to question the status quo and pursue my ideas.

I am indebted to the many economists, journalists and officials who have provided thoughts and insights for this book. Put two economists in a room and you end up with three opinions, they say. So I hope the finished product finds favour with at least one or two.

Of course, this book would have been a non-starter without the encouragement and endurance of my family and friends. Particular thanks to my father, Dr Paul David, for first inspiring me to take up economics. To my husband, Antony, for enabling me to take on this pet project. And to my daughters, for enduring months of rather distracted parenting and suggesting ideas for the cover. They even feigned an interest in central bank working papers (rather unnerving in a 6-year-old!). And finally to my mum, Ami, for teaching me that a woman can't be truly happy unless she's juggling at least eight things simultaneously, preferably at 4 a.m.

Index